SHOW
ME
HOW

S·E·R·I·E·S

SHOW ME HOW TO
ANSWER TOUGH
QUESTIONS

R. Larry Moyer

Kregel
Publications

Show Me How to Answer Tough Questions

© 1999 by R. Larry Moyer

Previously published as *Dear God, I'm Ticked Off*

Published by Kregel Publications, a division of Kregel, Inc., P.O. Box 2607, Grand Rapids, MI 49501.

Library of Congress Cataloging-in-Publication Data
Moyer, R. Larry (Richard Larry).
    Dear God, I'm ticked off: answering the spiritual complaints and concerns of others/ by R. Larry Moyer.
        p.   cm.
    1. Christianity—Miscellanea. 2. Spiritual life—Christianity—Miscellanea. I. Title.
BR96.M69   1999   230—dc 21   98-53733

ISBN 978-0-8254-3879-0

Printed in the United States of America

09 10 11 12 13 / 5 4 3 2 1

This book is dedicated to those
who are struggling
with honest and sincere questions
and to the Christians
who care enough to help them.

Contents

CONTENTS

Acknowledgments

There is no way this book would have been possible without the help of gifted and godly servants.

I am deeply grateful to Joy Kupp for her assistance in typing and retyping the manuscript. Her ability to type faster than I can even think is awesome. Her patience in reading my handwriting makes my debt to her enormous.

My thanks to Julie Boudreaux, Dennis Hillman, Marsha Marlowe, and Annette Scott for the tremendous feedback they gave me. Their comments made this a much better book.

I owe much to Adria Ger for her editing expertise and the way she so cheerily goes about helping.

There is no way I could ever thank the entire EvanTell staff enough for the way they have freed me up to do the only things I ever care to do—introduce people to our tremendous Savior and train others to do the same.

You make it such a delight to serve the Savior, to serve you, and to serve the many people who have never met Jesus Christ and have no idea what they are missing.

Part I

What Thirty-Five Years Has Taught Me

What Thirty-Five Years Has Taught Me

When I find something more exciting than what I am now doing, I'm going to go do it! But I don't expect I will. I don't know of anything more exciting than introducing people to Jesus Christ and training other believers to do the same thing. If you introduce others to Jesus Christ, your life takes on eternal significance. You've been used to populate heaven. And because eternal life is as secure as the promises of God, nobody can undo what God has used you to do. When you train other believers to do the same, you'll multiply yourself thousands of times over and will populate heaven many times faster. Thousands of believers will be helping you tell others, people you alone could never have reached. If that's not exciting, please tell me what is!

Having evangelized for longer than thirty-five years now, I'm bothered immensely by something. I can honestly say it has kept me awake at night. Most believers never lead anyone to Christ in their entire lives. Some surveys reveal that as few as 5 percent of believers lead people to Christ. Why don't the other 95 percent? I promise you, it's not because they don't want to. I've had too many people tell me how they have dreamed of leading even one person to Christ in their lifetime. Instead, one of the biggest reasons they give for their inactivity in evangelism is, "I'm afraid I won't be able to answer the questions and objections non-Christians have." They are referring to such questions and objections as "I don't believe the Bible," "Christians are hypocrites," "I don't believe there is a God," and so on.

But do you know what bothers me even more? When considering this problem—their inability to answer the questions and objections of non-Christians—believers make so many mistakes and have so many fallacies in their thinking. These mistakes and fallacies allow fear, rather than boldness, to have the upper hand. Let's talk about a few of them.

One mistake is to think that to reach a non-Christian, you have to be an intellectual giant—a person who can refute any question and respond to any objection. In other words, you have to be the equivalent of a seminary professor or have the mind of a C. S. Lewis.

What's wrong with that kind of thinking? I'm a graduate of both a college and a seminary. I know how to give all the arguments about the existence of God, explain all the apparent contradictions in the Bible, and analyze all the "theories" behind the empty tomb of Christ. But having interacted with non-Christians for over twenty-five years, I've found that often they didn't need intellectual answers. They needed common-sense answers—the kind that even a new believer in Christ could give. Those common-sense answers have done more to help me lead people to Christ than all the lectures I've heard in seminary classrooms, grateful though I am for the benefit of such training.

This willingness to provide common-sense answers is one reason new converts often lead more individuals to Christ than anyone else. It's not intellectual ability that's needed most in evangelism, it's enthusiasm and common sense empowered by the Holy Spirit. Dawson Trotman, founder of the Navigators, was right when he said, "Soul winners are not soul winners because of what they know but because of Who they know and how much they want others to know Him." Besides, when I do meet non-Christians who need someone with the mind of C. S. Lewis to speak to them, I know which books to loan them.

A second mistake believers make is that they too easily drift from the central message of Christianity—the substitutionary death of Christ and His resurrection on the third day. What God has done is irrefutable! Even though people are starving in third-world countries, even though children may die at an early age and adults can suffer agonizing deaths, how can I accuse Him of not being a God of love when He died on a cross for me? He did for me what I wouldn't think of doing for others. He has far more cause to question me than I have to question Him. Furthermore, if people don't believe there was a historical Jesus who died for them, they then have to explain away the empty tomb—one of the most attested facts of history! So with non-Christians I must keep going back to the cross and the empty tomb. Those are the issues. If He died for me, what am I going to do with Him? If He didn't arise the third day, disprove the empty tomb. Along with emphasizing the cross and the empty tomb, we must make it clear that we are saved simply by trusting in Jesus Christ as the only way to heaven. We can go through the motions, but if our trust is not in Christ alone to save us, we are lost. Many who sit in church every Sunday have missed that message!

A third mistake is taking the defensive instead of the offensive. It dawned on me after years in evangelism that God's greatest need was not the person who could defend Him but the one who would declare Him. After all, He is big enough to defend Himself! What I needed to do was take the offensive, not the defensive. It was so freeing and so illuminating to discover that truth. I don't have to have all the answers, I just have to be sure I have the correct message: Christ died for you and rose again. In fact, unbelievers have a bigger problem than I do. I have to explain what this God who exists is like. They have to explain what this God, who in their minds does not exist, is like! That's tough to do! Often when they do explain what He's like, I can say, "Okay, I don't think that person exists either." Then I tell them about the One who does exist—and the God of love He is.

Do you know what else astonished me? After years of studying the Scriptures, I was overwhelmed to find that all the things I was discovering from personal experience were taught in the examples and exhortations of Scripture. For example, when Paul the apostle entered Corinth—a city filled with philosophers and intellectuals dedicated to discussion and debate—he explains what he did. He states, "And I, brethren, when I came to you, did not come with excellence of speech or of wisdom declaring to you the testimony of God. For I determined not to know anything among you except Jesus Christ and Him crucified" (1 Cor. 2:1–2). Three verses later, he explains why: ". . . that your faith should not be in the wisdom of men but in the power of God."

Paul didn't want anyone leaving his presence saying, "I believe because Paul convinced me." He wanted everyone leaving to be able to say, "I believe because God convinced me." He knew that, ultimately, intellectual arguments and spiritual debates do not bring people to Christ. Only the Holy Spirit can do that. And when the Holy Spirit decides to work in a person's life—watch out! Similarly, when Paul entered Athens, confronted the philosophers, and faced a city "given over to idols" (Acts 17:16), what are we told he did? The text tells us "he preached to them Jesus and the resurrection" (v. 18).

For that reason I've had a passion to write a book that illustrates the way we ought to respond to non-Christians, based on how I would see God responding to their questions and struggles. No one, including me, can presume to speak on behalf of God. By writing such a book, I am not pretending to have such knowledge or ability. What is expressed here is based on my experience as an evangelist committed to the expositional handling of Scripture, and on my years of interaction with the struggles of non-Christians. The techniques presented here show how we can respond to non-Christians based on the way I would envision a loving God responding. Evangelism, biblically defined, is not just reaching the lost, but also it is equipping believers to evangelize. I trust that what I have to say will be of some help in equipping you to reach your non-Christian acquaintances.

With each individual presented in this book, I encourage

you to do three things. First, listen to what is being said. Each letter represents a struggle that a non-Christian is expressing to a person who has begun to talk to him or her about spiritual things. Then look carefully at what the non-Christian is expressing; this often reveals some common-sense issues we need to address. Third, respond the way you might envision a loving God responding. In each chapter the responder represents us as believers (whether our name be Kathy, Susan, Chip, or Jack), and the response is the reply we ought to give to non-Christians.

As I write these responses, I demonstrate how we must keep going back to the cross and the resurrection. And by the way, here's where I need your understanding. You may read about four chapters and feel like shouting, "I've got it! Now I see how to keep taking the conversation back to the cross and the resurrection." For you I would not have to be as repetitive in the following chapters. I could simply come to a point and say, "Now do what I've just taught you to do." Others, who feel less confident in evangelism, have said to me, "Please don't assume anything. Keep showing me, conversation after conversation, how to go back to the cross and the empty tomb." For those people, I've done just that in every chapter. As I've done so, I've also tried to help believers understand the value of a compliment. Sincere compliments have a way of helping non-Christians relax and enjoy our conversations with them, making us seem less threatening to them.

I have a simple goal. It's not to give you pat answers to non-Christians' questions. If I attempted to do that, you'd often find yourself frustrated when one non-Christian didn't express his struggle or question the same way as another did, and the answer you had prepared simply didn't fit. Instead, I want to help you learn how to listen and then how to think before responding to non-Christians—how to think in a biblical, common-sense way. If you learn how to listen and how to think, you will be able to answer any non-Christian anywhere, and you will find yourself freed up in evangelism, no longer intimidated by what an unbeliever might ask or say.

John 1:14 tells us that Jesus Christ was "full of grace and truth." We need that same balance. Some believers have grace but little or no truth in their response to non-Christians. Hence, they never confront the non-Christian with the truth of his sinful condition before God. Others have truth but no grace. Their cold, caustic, callous way of responding to non-Christians often leaves the unbeliever with little interest in Christ or Christianity. We need grace accompanied by truth and truth accompanied by grace. I trust the responses in the following chapters reveal that kind of balance.

One more thing—something I want to say loudly and clearly. Please don't think for half a second that I believe people are brought to Christ through our well-thought-out answers or responses. Nothing could be further from the truth. One of my favorite verses throughout my ministry has been John 6:44, which says, "No one can come to me unless the Father who sent Me draws him." I believe God wants us to develop and improve our communication skills, thereby increasing our effectiveness in helping lost people understand the gospel. But never lose sight of the fact that it is God who brings people to Christ. What God is asking you to do is bring Christ to your non-Christian acquaintances.

If in reading this book you find yourself freed up and fired up to talk to non-Christians and aggressively pursue them for Christ, the time spent in writing it was well worth the effort. Again I ask, What on earth could be more exciting than being used by God to populate heaven?

Part 2

Letters

Matt's Struggle

God may have created the world,
but circumstantial evidence proves he
doesn't know how to run it.

Who Is Matt?

Matt is an upper-middle-class insurance company executive who lives in Dallas, Texas. He is in his midforties, happily married, and the father of three children. He has provided well for their needs and prides himself on being a successful businessman with a good reputation in the community. When approached about spiritual things, he admits being annoyed with the "injustices" surrounding life. If he has such a concern for his family, why can God not have that same concern for His world?

Listening to Matt

Dear Mike,

If I were you, I'd be embarrassed. God makes such lofty claims of might and power, but it appears he's lost control. Sometimes it would be easy to convince me he made the world. All the other explanations for how the universe got started don't particularly impress me, even though at times I pretend they do. But, pardon my bluntness, I often feel that any ten-year-old with brains could run things better than God has.

Take, for example, one of the worst mass murders in U.S. history, the one that occurred in Killeen, Texas. Living here in Dallas, I saw that really shook up a lot of people. Some people have probably forgotten it by now, but I haven't. A guy drove his pickup through the front window of a cafeteria at lunchtime, pulled out a gun, opened fire, then turned the gun on himself. God just stood there with his arms folded. He could have prevented the whole thing—yet he did absolutely nothing. That incident alone did not win him a lot of support.

That tragedy was not nearly as bad as the bombing of the Federal Building in Oklahoma City. There's something nobody will forget. I visited my stepfather, who lives there, two weeks after the bombing. I saw the damage as well as the memorials to all the innocent little children who died along with so many, many adults. As far as I am concerned, the entire scene had evidence of an uncaring God written all over it. The whole time I stood there and looked at the ruins, I kept asking, "Why did this have to happen? Why didn't God prevent it?"

There are times I try to be fair and say what I often hear Christians say: "Don't blame that on God. It just shows you how wicked men are." But how do you account for those things that nobody denies are "acts of God?" For example, what about Hurricane Andrew, which became the costliest natural disaster in U.S. history? Deaths, missing people, destroyed homes, rat infestations—the list goes on and on. One paper reported that two hundred fifty thousand people were left homeless, ten thousand dwellings were destroyed, and another seventy-five thousand houses were damaged. Does God enjoy seeing that kind of devastation? I still remember that one of the people killed in Louisiana was a two-year-old girl. What could she possibly have done for God to punish her in that way? Why didn't he prevent the whole thing?

On the world scene, things are even worse. The starvation occurring in some countries is mind-boggling. People are dying by the thousands. In other countries, one tyrant can slaughter hundreds in a day. These countries face violence even more than hunger. There are times I'm not a very caring person, but even I want to reach out and help. God could help, but he doesn't. And then he calls me a sinner?

Mike, face it. God doesn't make sense.

Matt

Looking at Matt

Matt is being totally human. The nature of his letter tells me that Matt sees what is wrong with others a lot more quickly than what is wrong with himself. Even when he admits his own weaknesses and failures, he makes only a passing reference to them, such as when he says, "There are times I'm not a very caring person, but even I want to reach out and help." The "but" in his sentence tells me he is probably an individual who, like most other people, would have difficulty admitting to himself that he is a sinner. That is especially clear when he adds, "And then He calls me a sinner?"

Matt has done what many non-Christians do—they see the side of God they are looking for, even if it is a side that does not exist. Most of us are accusatory by nature. Our depravity finds pointing out what's wrong with people more enjoyable than pointing out what's right. That way of thinking often affects us when it comes to our spiritual perspective.

In pondering who God is and what He is like, Matt needs to start with the cross. Anyone who would give eternal life absolutely free has a lot of kindness about Him. There is no greater way God could have become involved than to allow His perfect Son to die on the cross as our substitute. If a man's character is being questioned, he will often reveal any noble or charitable act he has done. Presidential candidates accused of being cold or uncaring do this. They have family members or close associates speak of their benevolent deeds or kind acts. Similarly, before we become too critical of what we feel God has done in the present, consistency demands that we look at what He has done in the past. Why not allow God the same privilege we would extend to anybody else?

Matt does what most people do—he takes the short-range view of life. The issue is not "Will hatred and all wrong-doing be punished?" The only question is, "When?" Non-Christians who are not accustomed to thinking with eternity in view often have little or no concept that a future day of judgment is coming. Even if they see themselves having to answer to God for what they've done, and many of them do, they think little of how a future day of judgment will affect other people and the world scene.

Responding to Matt

Dear Matt,

You are tempted to think I don't understand, but I assure you, I do. Please don't accuse God of not caring. Just because He doesn't intervene in world events doesn't mean He doesn't care. Any injustice or hardship grieves Him more than it does anyone else. He was even grieved the other day, Matt, when you cussed out your neighbor for damaging the electric saw you loaned him. Do you remember telling me how you felt? Yet even you thought it was possible that the saw had been damaged when you gave it to him. And even if he had broken it, did it really call for that kind of reaction? Like the rest of us, you often see how, in your opinion, God has mishandled situations, but see none of your mishandling of your own life. As you know, I'm not a morning person. The first two hours of every day I'm horrible to be around. Whenever I think how irritated God ought to be about the wrongs I see in the world, I'm reminded how He would have every right to be irritated with my 7 to 9 A.M. performances.

Matt, if you saw world events through God's eyes, your view would be so different. Even if He tried to explain things to you, you wouldn't understand. His mind is so beyond anything ours is capable of comprehending. If it weren't, He wouldn't be God. The fact that there are things you don't understand about what He does and allows ought to impress you rather than depress you.

Let me point out something rather simple. You know through your own experience that you always see in a person what you want to see. Even though God's character is beyond reproach, if you want to find a wrong side of Him, one way or another, you'll find it. But why not give Him credit for what He's done right? You have three very intelligent children. Have you ever asked, "Why should I be given these wonderful children when some couples can't have any?" Your wife worships you, and even you would admit you don't always deserve that. I'll bet there are times, when you are alone, that you realize what a selfish person you are. I can tell by some of the comments you've made to me. Have you ever asked yourself, "If there is a God, why would He allow me to have such a loyal wife?"

Even at work you have been fortunate. You find your job satisfying, and you're one of few people who feel secure in your position. Yet you usually see the bad side of everyone. I wish sometimes you'd look for the good side. I challenge you to list everything good in your life and place it alongside everything you feel God's done wrong. Hopefully, you will discover you don't applaud Him where, in fact, He deserves applause.

Nothing I've said concerns me more than what I am about to ask you to consider. When pondering how good God is, please start with the cross. He's written three verses in the Bible that have helped a lot of people in this area. They are found in a book called Romans in the New Testament portion of the Bible. In the fifth chapter of Romans and beginning in the sixth verse you will read, "For when we were still without strength, in due time Christ died for the ungodly. For scarcely for a righteous man will one die; yet perhaps for a good man someone would even dare to die. But God demonstrates His own love toward us, in that while we were still sinners, Christ died for us." Would you allow me to ask you a question? You referred to the massacre in Texas, where a man gunned down a lunchtime crowd of innocent people. Suppose that man had not killed himself but, instead, had fled the crime scene, was later captured, tried for his crime, and sentenced to die for it. If it were possible, would you die as his substitute? I'm sure you would say, "No way." I can't say I would either.

Yet that is exactly what God's Son Jesus Christ did. He died for sinners—people who were completely undeserving, like you and me. Why? So that when He had paid for your sin, and risen the third day, He could forgive you for all of the wrongs you've done and give you, completely free, His gift of eternal life. All people need to do is come to Him as a sinner, recognize that His Son was their substitute on the cross, and trust in Christ alone to save them. From that point on, they are forever His. Since God allowed His Son to take the place of all sinners on a cross so they could live with Him forever, doesn't that remove all doubt about His character? Who else would die for you except someone who loves you that much? When His Son stretched out His arms and died for us, that removed all questions about His concern. Since you and I know that we would not do the same thing, He has every right to question our character. We have no reason to question His. Anyone who would let His Son die for you does not mean you any harm. Now you know why a person once expressed it by saying, "He's too loving to do you wrong; He's too wise to make a mistake."

You mentioned the tyrant who slaughters hundreds of people. Don't think God is standing by unaware. If that tyrant does not come to Christ, his punishment awaits him. The Bible clearly declares in the twentieth chapter of Revelation, "Anyone not found written in the Book of Life was cast into the lake of fire." In an eternal hell, he will wish to die but won't be able to. Just look at the world around you. Every day people rebel and get further away from God. Until Christ returns to earth, the situation will get worse, not better. My wife and I were talking the other night about the increase in violence in the last twenty years. Left to itself, humanity will do wrong, not right. God could step in and stop it, and one day He is going to do just that. But keep in mind, He's a Savior, not a dictator. He's given everyone a choice. They can come to Him, receive forgiveness for all their sins, and live in eternity with Him. Or they can choose to reject Him and live a life independent of Him, a life that becomes more miserable with each step. And the most miserable thing of all will be to be separated from Him forever. The choice is theirs to make.

You are probably saying, "But you still have not addressed the issue. What about the victims of those disasters and violence?" That is why God pleads with people to come to Christ now. Until He establishes a new world, there will always be violence. Please remember that He has not rebelled against men; men have rebelled against Him. In their rebellion, they do things that are wicked, and innocent people become victims. Don't forget, my own brother was killed in a car accident when he was hit head-on by a drunk driver. God has proven His love for those victims the same way He proved His love for those who committed the violence. Christ died for their sins, too. What greater way is there to "get involved?" Quite frankly, Matt, that's why I try to talk to as many people as I can about spiritual things. Unfortunately, not all of them are as willing to ask questions as you are. When people come to Christ, even if they are the victims of the worst violence, they will live with Him forever. That is the ultimate joy. Several of the people who died in Killeen were undoubtedly His people. If only they all had been.

I assure you, Matt, according to the Bible a day is coming when the earth will know no violence. There will be no suffering, shootings, hijackings, famine, catastrophes, pain, or hardship of any kind. All those who know Him will be together with Him in eternal bliss. When they see things from

His perspective, they will realize how just and righteous He's been and is. God really wants you in His family.

Thanks for listening, Matt. I do appreciate you. Let's keep the lines of communication open, okay? Tell Jennifer and the kids I said hello.

Mike

Kellie's Struggle

How can I trust a book that was written
over two thousand years ago?
Besides that, the Bible could win a prize
for being one of the most boring books
ever written.

Who Is Kellie?

Kellie is a third-year graduate student in business at the University of Illinois. Her parents, although claiming to be Christians and wanting to be thought of as such, never understood the Christian message and went to church only when it was convenient. Kellie is an avid reader but has a limited attention span. If she doesn't find something interesting, she quickly drops it. She also is quite trusting, and readily accepts most of what she hears. She is more interested in things that are current than things she deems outdated.

Listening to Kellie

Dear Joy,

My friends tell me God can do the impossible. At times they sound pretty convincing. Admittedly, something has happened in my friend Jenny's life. There used to be only two things she lived for: sex and drugs. We had plenty of both in Chicago where we grew up. When she made a 180-degree turn, most people thought she'd gone a little weird. At least she's not wasting her life like a lot of people are. I really don't know what happened six months ago. I do know that's when she started smiling for the first time. She gives the credit to God. She is such a different person now. Her life is a complete contrast to what it was her senior year in high school.

But that's not what I want to talk about. Here's my problem. Sometimes I think that God not only does the impossible, he expects the impossible. Take his book, the Bible. It was written so many years ago it's outdated. You told me the other day, "Just read the Bible, Kellie, and find out for yourself." But I don't see how you can expect me to trust a book that's so old. My professors at the university don't help a lot. Most of them snicker at the idea that a person would even read the Bible, let alone trust it. They love to refer to its many contradictions.

That's not my only problem with the Bible. About three years ago I really panicked when the doctor thought he spotted a tumor during a routine checkup. It turned out to be nothing, but for a few days I really got serious about death, not that I ever did take it lightly. I picked up a Bible my folks have. I read a few chapters—I don't even know what part I read. I didn't understand a word it was saying, and I was really bored. I was glad I'd had a good night's sleep before I started reading, or it would have put me to sleep in a hurry. I know I'm probably sounding sarcastic, but I'm wondering if reading the Bible is part of the punishment we have to endure if we want to go to heaven. If so, I don't know if I can take it. Does God ever make exceptions? I went to church two Sundays in a row when I had that cancer scare. I honestly tried to give the preacher a chance, but he was as confusing and boring as the Bible. Sometimes I wonder if he has the same struggles with the Bible that I do.

Is there something I'm missing? If there is, please tell me what it is.

Kellie

Looking at Kellie

Kellie's entire struggle, in many respects, is with the Scriptures. In this, she puts the cart before the horse.

To help Kellie, we need to point out several things. First, she needs to understand that the truth about Christ does not stand or fall with the Bible. The Bible is indeed a book without error or mistake. But to argue that at this juncture would be a moot point. Kellie needs to understand that the Bible simply tells about the Christ of Christianity. Christianity, though, stands or falls with the empty tomb. Kellie must therefore be challenged to learn about the empty tomb. Because of the empty tomb, even if there were no Bible, every person still would have to deal with the Person of Jesus Christ.

Even the miracles of the Bible are not the issue. Christ is! He is the one who performed the miracles. So the issue non-Christians must continually address is, Who is Jesus Christ? That is why, when non-Christians do study the Bible, they must be encouraged to start with the gospel of John, the one book of the Bible specifically written for non-Christians. The book of John testifies to who Jesus Christ is and calls upon all people to put their faith in Him as their only access to eternal life.

To help Kellie, we also need to take the offensive, not the defensive. Where are the "contradictions" in the Bible? Has anyone disproved the empty tomb of Christ? Unless we take the offensive, Kellie will not be challenged to think for herself.

Being such a trusting person, Kellie also needs to come to grips with the fact that just because someone like a professor is right on one thing does not mean he is right on everything. Properly pointing out that simple truth to Kellie may compel her to consider everything she hears before accepting it as truth.

It is most important to observe the "clues" Kellie provides. Most non-Christians drop ideas or thoughts that are troubling them when they engage in conversation. Sometimes these "clues" are about what they have told you, and at other times they are about what they haven't told you. Kellie's comment, "At least she's not wasting her life like a lot of people are," is quite revealing. She obviously thinks quite deeply about her life and is an intense kind of person. The fact that she is a third-year graduate student in business at the University of Illinois would also indicate that. This intensity makes her take life very seriously, even more so after her cancer scare. Here is something that could help her go beyond thinking about the Bible to her personal need of Christ.

Responding to Kellie

Dear Kellie,

You're not the first one to struggle with the Bible. Join the club! I struggled there for years. One of the biggest complaints people have about the Bible is that it is so old and boring. Let me try to explain things the best I can. Thanks for sharing your true feelings with me. I'll never think less of you because of anything you ask, even if you disagree with me.

You're right, Kellie. The Bible is an old book. In fact, it was written over a fifteen-hundred-year span of time covering forty generations. But the fact that it's old doesn't mean it's not reliable. Sometimes things that are around the longest deserve the most attention. They have stood the test of time. At the university I attended in Florida, there were professors like yours who had absolutely no regard for the Bible and degraded it in class. But I had one professor who did respect it. Why? Rather than reading the Bible with a closed mind, he studied its reliability objectively. I wish you could talk with him—he would enthusiastically tell you what he discovered. He would share some facts that would surprise you and mean a lot to you.

For example, the Bible is divided into Old and New Testament sections. Do you realize that, although we do not have the original documents of the New Testament, there are more than twenty-four thousand manuscript copies of portions of the New Testament? Not one ancient book has that many copies surviving. Not one! So, in all fairness, if we are going to question the reliability of the Bible, should we not question even more the reliability of other ancient writing we've studied? My point, Kellie, is that just because the Bible is old is no reason to doubt its trustworthiness.

Take the Bible at face value for a moment. If you do, you will discover that God used more than forty writers. And remember, He did this over a fifteen-hundred-year span. Those men were not writing from hearsay. Either they were actual eyewitnesses or they were writing about firsthand information. Jesus Christ walked and ate with men such as Matthew, Mark, Luke, and John and appeared personally to Paul. They listened and spoke to Jesus and heard firsthand what He taught. By the way, these men were respected in their own fields. Not one of them had a reputation for lying or distorting the truth. If they had lied, don't you think the people within their own community would have pointed out inaccuracies? People of their day had good minds just like yours, Kellie. They accepted the Bible as truth. Many of them had seen what the writers of the Bible wrote, and they knew it was accurate.

Just consider the fact that more than forty authors wrote over the course of forty generations, and they all recorded the same thing! Some of these writers were what you would call blue-collar workers, and others were white-collar workers. Not once in the entire Bible do any of them contradict each other. That, in itself, shows a divine force was behind what they were writing.

I know what you're thinking: "But my professors say the Bible is loaded with contradictions." Ask them to show you one. Even things they could point to as contradictions are revealed not to be when the Bible is studied honestly and objectively. Sometimes they are nothing more than two men reporting the same event from two different perspectives. In addition, there's something your professors aren't telling you. Not one thing they consider to be a contradiction deals with a major truth. Their "contradictions" never deal with issues that are of eternal consequence.

Don't think that I dislike or lack respect for your professors. The fact is, I do respect them in many areas. But how do you know if they're being completely honest with you? Bear in mind that you are a trusting individual. Couldn't it be that any one of them has times of uncertainty about what he's just taught you or even how the Bible could affect his life? Don't make your professors into some kind of super-humans who are right on everything. As I mentioned, I had professors in Florida who did the same thing—snickered at the Bible. One of them was a professor whose marriage was on the rocks. His whole life has since gone to pieces. I just found out that his wife left him and took the children with her. I had wanted to talk to him about spiritual matters, but I think he sensed what I wanted to discuss and avoided me at all costs.

Kellie, let me explain something else that most people don't ever think about. What parts of the Bible do people question the most? They're stories such as Jonah and the fish—or the whale, as people define the fish. Do you know who referred to that particular story more than anyone else? It was Jesus Christ. So, ultimately, every question about the Bible comes back to the basic question: "Who is Jesus Christ?" The truth of Christianity does not stand or fall with the Bible. The Bible simply talks about the truth of Christianity. The truth of Christianity ultimately stands or falls with Jesus Christ. Was He the One He said He was?

Whenever anyone questions the authority of the Bible, I challenge them to study the empty tomb of Christ—the proof that He is the Son of God. The empty tomb happens to be one of the most historically documented facts of history. Historical facts, apart from from those in the Bible, have proven that the grave was empty on the third day. Nobody, including skeptics, have succeeded in disproving His resurrection. You have such a good mind. I'd encourage you to make that same investigation. If you do, you will see that Jesus Christ is who He claimed to be—the One sent by God. So the next time someone goes on an endless tirade about the Bible, remind him or her that even if the Bible did not exist they would still have to deal with who Jesus Christ is and the abundant evidence behind the empty tomb.

Now let's talk about the Bible being, as you called it, "boring." At least you are not afraid to call it that. Too many people think of God as somebody who will strike them dead if they say something like that. He's never yet struck anyone dead for such a remark. If He did, I would have died years ago.

You've always been one to put the cart before the horse. Do you remember the time you decided to get a college education? Being your enthusiastic self, you immediately wrote six letters to six major universities and asked them for a catalog. Then your dad, who knows you better than you think he does, asked you two very simple questions: "What do you want to be?" and "What course of studies do you want to pursue?" Do you remember our laughing about that together? You had gotten so excited about college that you failed to put first things first. As your dad pointed out, it's not what they have to offer, it's what you want to study and prepare to be. That's only one example. I could add a lot more.

What am I getting at? There will always be parts of the Bible you don't understand. Concern yourself with the parts you do understand. Begin reading the fourth book of the New Testament portion of the Bible. It's called John. You will find a lot in that book that is very understandable. Why start there? Because that book tells you how you can know Christ as your personal Savior. Begin with the first chapter. Don't do what so many others do and start in the middle. The Bible is the best literature ever written, and all of the sixty-six books should be studied the same way you study any great literature. Each book should be read from beginning to end, not by starting in the middle. Furthermore, once you come to Christ, and I so hope you do, God comes to you in what the Bible calls the Person of the Holy Spirit. The Holy Spirit will enable you to understand parts of the Bible you never understood before. That is why some of your friends who are Christians get so excited about Bible study. They came to Christ, and through His Holy Spirit, God is helping them understand the Bible. They, like me, called it boring. Now they call it exciting.

Do you see what I mean about putting the cart before the horse? You first need to come to Christ. God wants to give you the free gift of eternal life. He gives it to anyone who will ask Him for it. Once He's on the inside of your life, you will understand parts of the Bible as you've never understood them before.

By the way, I agree that a lot of preachers are boring. Tell me about it! But God doesn't make preachers boring. Some preachers are boring for the same reason some of our professors were boring. Some preachers are serious, but they don't always know how to communicate effectively. Some don't study or develop their skills as they should. However, there are those who do speak in an interesting way that you can understand. Don't let Satan's use of uninteresting preachers make you reject Jesus Christ. Excuses will be of no consequence when each of us one day stands before God.

Speaking of standing before God, you said something that shows you still don't understand what I've been trying to say. You asked, "Is reading the Bible part of the punishment a person has to endure if he wants to go to heaven?" You keep missing the message, Kellie. I realize in some ways you're kidding, but there is no punishment we have to endure to get to heaven. Eternal life is a free gift. Why? Because God's Son has already taken the punishment for everything we've done wrong. He did not deserve to be nailed to a cross—but you and I do. You and I are the ones who have done wrong. He died for us. He was the only one who could have done so because He alone was perfect. One sinner cannot die for another sinner. Jesus Christ died for you and was victorious over sin and the grave through His resurrection on the third day. God can now forgive you all your wrongs and offer you, absolutely free, the gift of life eternal. That's why the book of John, which I've encouraged you to study, uses the word believe.

Do you remember when your car broke down on the way to the airport? You were close to missing your plane! I was frustrated that I couldn't get free from work to help you. A business associate of your dad's came along and offered you a ride. He even said he'd call your dad and take care of your car. What did you do? You trusted him—a person—to get you to the airport. Similarly, God is asking you to trust a Person—His Son Jesus Christ—as your only way to heaven. That's what believe means. When you trust God's Son as your only way to heaven, you are saying to God, "I accept what Jesus did as my only way to heaven." Instantly God will give you the free gift of life eternal. You are a morally good person. But you've still sinned. God cannot accept you based on your good works. He can only accept you based on what His Son did for you on the cross.

One more thing, Kellie. You said about Jennie, "At least she is not wasting her life like a lot of people are." Could we talk more about that sometime? Before I came to Christ my life was so empty. One day I even thought to myself, "I can understand why people commit suicide. There sure doesn't seem to be a whole lot to life." But since my college roommate introduced me to Christ, things have changed. For the first time ever, I feel like I'm living life instead of wasting it. If you had known me then, you'd understand.

You mentioned the scare you had with a possible tumor three years ago. I've never gone through anything like that, but it means a lot to me to know that if anything happened, I'd be with Christ forever. Even here on earth, Kellie, life is so different for me as a Christian. Now I feel I have a reason to get up in the morning. Before I trusted Christ, I just wanted to pull the covers over my head and pretend life wasn't there. What a change! You take life and death very seriously. With Christ, you could have the answer to both.

Please come to Christ, Kellie. Then let Him help you enjoy the Bible. I promise you, my whole attitude about the

Bible changed when I became a Christian, and yours will, too. You won't feel like you're reading somebody else's mail any longer.

Joy

letter three

Lindsey's Struggle

*Some of the things that God has done
are gross or just plain bizarre.
Why was bloodshed so necessary?*

Who Is Lindsey?

Lindsey is the mother of two children. She has a part-time job and lives in Colorado. Having grown up in a God-fearing home, she is familiar with the Bible. One thing that has bothered her for years, though, is the "bloodthirstiness" behind the cross. Her husband, an electrician, would easily come to Christ if Lindsey would, but being a passive individual, he is waiting for her to get her struggle resolved.

Listening to Lindsey

Dear Julie,

Sometimes the things God has done seem not only strange but bordering on gross—or even bizarre. I wonder at times if he's not too focused on bloodshed. Wayne is probably tired of hearing me talk about this, though he listens. But this issue bothers me.

I have heard Jesus Christ referred to as God's Son. My stepdad, who talked to me about spiritual things, said Jesus was the only Son God had. He tried to explain things about Jesus' birth that I still don't understand, but that's not what troubles me. What bothers me is that he said Jesus Christ's death on the cross was part of God's plan. To deal with my sin, God had to punish his Son. Why should the innocent have to pay for the guilty? Besides that, if I had only one son, I sure wouldn't kill him. I don't understand why my sin has to be "paid for." But even if it does, if God is so wise and intelligent, couldn't he have come up with a better solution?

I'm a young mother with two children. They are so special to me and always will be. I would never let them pay for what somebody else did, and under no circumstances would I ever kill them. The thought of that makes me sick. It brings tears to my eyes when I read in the newspaper about a parent killing a child. It takes me weeks to forget the story. This might be a terrible thing to say but I'm going to say it. Sometimes, when I think of what God did when he killed Jesus, I wonder if I don't know more about love than he does. Oh, I know you're probably going to tell me the same thing my stepdad did: God didn't kill Jesus; he just let him be killed. But as far as I'm concerned, it makes absolutely no difference. He still killed him.

Don't I have a right to feel the way I do?

Lindsey

Looking at Lindsey

There aren't multiple struggles keeping Lindsey from Christ, there is just a single issue: the seeming bloodthirstiness of God in allowing His Son to die on a cross.

It would do little good to try to persuade Lindsey that she is looking at things from the wrong perspective for two reasons. First, to the natural mind, that is the way it seems. Couldn't God have planned another way to redeem the world? Second, that is the way she feels, and she has as much right to her own thoughts and feelings as anybody else.

But the most important issue is this: Why try to talk her out of her perspective when the blood Christ shed on the cross is the loudest and clearest way God could say "I love you"? Often believers feel they must make excuses for God when the very thing they are worried about, if it's examined properly, actually commends His character. Lindsey's concern over the blood shed at the cross is a tremendous opportunity to applaud His character and His love.

People identify with the newspaper. Many read it every day. Using current events to illustrate biblical truth is highly effective. Equally effective is the use of illustrations from daily life that others can identify with.

It is encouraging when non-Christians have a single issue before them. If that issue is addressed, as the Holy Spirit works in them they can quickly see their need to trust Christ.

Responding to Lindsey

Dear Lindsey,

It seems to me that you're really asking two questions, and, as usual, you get right to the point. I'm glad you do.

Your first question—Why does sin have to be paid for?—is one of the hardest things to grasp. Because our nature differs so much from God's, that is understandable. Thanks for hearing me out, though, because I want to help.

You have never denied making mistakes or doing wrong. Nobody has to convince you that you are a sinner; you're harder on yourself than anyone else is. But the fact is, you and I are human and we do sin. The very nature of God, though, is intrinsically holy. He has never sinned, and the thought of sin never enters His mind. His holiness is such that He cannot do wrong.

That's why sin must be punished. If God tolerated sin we could appropriately accuse Him of being anything but holy. In fact, we could rightly call Him a hypocrite. But the fact that He cannot allow sin in His presence attests to His holiness.

I'd like to use two "homey" illustrations to help you

understand. Lindsey, you're an immaculate housekeeper. Anyone who knows you well can testify to that. I told Louie the other day, "I sure wish I could keep this house the way Lindsey keeps hers." When we stopped by on vacation last year, you told us you tidied up because we were coming. But Louie and I knew the truth. Your house is always ready for company. Despite having two children and a part-time job, you take pride in keeping your house neat and clean. Your kitchen floor is swept regularly and polished often. Remember the time your neighbor teased you about being able to eat dinner off your floor? That would probably be true all the time if it weren't for your son, Jonathan. The prints he sometimes leaves with his muddy shoes can be a sight to behold! You've told me what happens at those times—you lose your temper! As you said just the other day, your blood pressure rises and so does your voice. Remember the time he said to you, "Mom, couldn't you just remind me without yelling at me?" You and I are a lot alike. That's probably one reason we enjoy each other's company. You know that when something like that happens to me, I can become downright angry!

Why do you lose your temper? It's not because you don't love Jonathan. It's because his muddy shoes don't go with something as beautiful as your floor. A spot of dirt on something so spotless repulses you. Similarly, on a higher, much more important level, someone as holy as God cannot allow something as awful as sin. Even the smallest sin is repulsive to Him. The holiness of His character demands that sin be punished. Anything less would mean that He's not the just God He's declared Himself to be. A holy God who desires to be just has to reward righteousness and punish sin. The punishment for sin is death and, ultimately, eternal separation from Him.

Here's a second illustration that might help. Two years ago, just before our two families went on that picnic in the mountains together, you were summoned for jury duty. A middle-aged man had committed armed robbery at a convenience store there in Colorado Springs. The prosecuting attorney presented his case and left the defense attorney few options.

Everything, from the witnesses who saw the defendant running from the store to the store's security camera, proved the police had captured the right man. You told us after the trial how repentant the man seemed. He cried during the sentencing phase when he told the jury of the dire family circumstances that drove him to commit robbery. Yet you not only found him guilty, you voted in favor of a heavy sentence. Couldn't you just have excused him and forgotten about it? No, because you are a law-abiding citizen and our government requires that crime be punished. Remember our talking about that?

To a far greater degree, God's holiness demands that sin be punished. Holiness cannot tolerate it or make excuses for it. Holiness must punish sin. As the Bible says, "The wages of sin is death." That is a simple and necessary truth.

The second question you're asking is, Why would God kill Jesus to punish sin? This is going to surprise you, but I agree with you. The issue is not whether God killed Jesus or let Him be killed. Either way, God was in the driver's seat. He was responsible for Jesus' death.

What you don't realize is that you've answered your own question. You mentioned that you couldn't kill your child. That shows you the depth of His love versus yours and mine. Somebody might say to you, "I love you. Here's my house. I'll give it to you." But how do you know that person doesn't own ten homes so that giving up one is no sacrifice? Another person could say to you, "I love you. Here's a million dollars." But how do you know he is not a billionaire? When God says, "I love you. Here's My perfect and only Son," that is love. The greatest proof of His love is that He would allow His Son, Jesus Christ, to die for your sins. That's why I keep referring to a verse in the Bible that says, "For God so loved the world that He gave His only begotten Son, that whoever believes in Him should not perish but have everlasting life." It's the sixteenth verse of the third chapter of John.

Remember reading in your newspaper about the seventeen-year-old girl, Tonya Farmer, who died saving others? Louie told me the two of you were talking about it. During an apartment fire, Tonya handed her two- and four-year-old nieces to a neighbor through an upstairs window. As the papers reported it, she was trying to rescue another niece and a friend when she collapsed from smoke inhalation. Why did she do that? My husband showed me the newspaper clipping. A person who knew her well said, "She was the sweetest person. She loved those little girls [her nieces] to death." Because of the even greater love God has for you, He allowed His Son to die in your place. Because Jesus did that, God can completely forgive you for all your wrongs.

As God has promised, He will give you eternal life absolutely free if, as a sinner, you will trust Him as your personal Savior. He is asking you to depend on Christ in simple faith as your only way to heaven. That's why He pleads with us to come to Him and let Him forgive us and save us from our sins. He wants you and me with Him forever. The fact that He would allow a perfect Son to die for us and take the punishment for our sins proves that.

Could He have allowed somebody else to die? Sure! But it would have had to be somebody who was perfect. A sinner cannot die for a sinner any more than an armed thief could pay for another armed thief's crime. His Son was the only perfect One there was. God could have kept Him in heaven and the two of them could have enjoyed that entire mansion for themselves. Instead, God let Christ die for you.

Let me share something else that might help. You use the word "kill." What you may not understand is that even though it was "God's plan," His Son Jesus chose to die. Christ's own love was revealed when He spoke of the oneness He and the Father have. As He said to His accusers, "Therefore My Father loves me, because I lay down My life that I may take it again. No one takes it from Me, but I lay it down of Myself. I have power to lay it down, and I have power to take it again." That's found in the same book of John in the Bible. When someone voluntarily wants to be a sacrifice for your sin, is that killing Him? Did someone kill Tonya? Or did Tonya, out of love, choose to die?

Whatever you do, don't overlook what you have every reason to be excited about. On the third day, as historical records prove, Jesus Christ rose supernaturally. When He did that, He proved He had conquered sin. Sin did not conquer Him. Anyone with the power to rise from the grave has proven His credentials. He is able to save you and give you eternal life.

God's justice says there is no sin so small that He can overlook it. His love says there is no sin so big that He cannot forgive it. Through the cross and the blood shed on it, God is saying, "I love you and I want you to be with Me forever."

I would be so happy to see you and Wayne resolve this whole issue and know you are His forever. I hope I've helped. Please let me know if I haven't. You won't hurt my feelings. I've tried to explain things the best I can. Our relationship means a lot to me, and I want to be here for you. You are a very sincere person with very sincere questions. I'll surprise you with a call one of these weekends, and we'll talk some more.

Julie

letter four

Chuck's Struggle

*I've discovered that those who do wrong
prosper, and those who do right suffer.
Because of this, I'd rather be a bad guy.*

Who Is Chuck?

Chuck lives in a suburb of Miami, Florida, with his wife and three children—a boy and two girls, all of them teenagers. He grew up in St. Louis, where his family belonged to a liberal church they rarely attended. His wife, also unaccustomed to church, respects him highly, and his entire family thinks and believes as he does. Chuck is more materialistic than he admits to being and only recently, through Carlton's witness, has begun to think about spiritual things.

Listening to Chuck

Dear Carlton,

The other day, we started to talk about spiritual things. I want to ask you something that has bothered me off and on for years. In a nutshell, I think God needs to get clear in his mind who the bad guys are and who the good guys are. Once he figures that out, he needs to back the side he's supposed to be on—that of the good guys.

My neighbor Jeff lives two doors down and is one of the greatest fellows God has working for him. Unlike a lot of people, he lives like a Christian. There's hardly a Sunday he isn't in church. But that's not what impresses me. What I most admire is that he's as consistent on Monday morning as he is on Sunday morning. Do you know what he and his family did last year? One day in July, my wife was running late for an appointment. The carpet on our stairs is slippery if your foot hits it at the wrong angle. As she rushed downstairs, she took a nasty fall and badly bruised her ankle. For six weeks she had to go everywhere on crutches. Jeff's wife, Tammy, saw her getting the mail and asked her what had happened. Within twenty-four hours, they brought over enough food for our entire day. That was only the first of four meals they brought us. One Saturday I had to work, and when I came home, my yard was mowed, edged, manicured—the whole works. It must have taken Jeff and his son at least two hours to do that. They left a note saying, "Chuck, we just wanted to help. You have enough to do with Sue being on crutches." I've never told anyone, but tears came to my eyes.

I don't know anybody who will do more for others than that family. They are a family anyone can count on if they need help. Jeff could run for mayor and win by a landslide.

But here's the kicker. For the last five years Jeff has known nothing but hardship. He's not had a job for more than a year and a half. As soon as he's at a job that long he's promoted. Then there's a layoff, downsizing, or something else, and he's let go. On one of his jobs with an engineering firm, the entire branch closed eighteen months after Jeff was hired. Tammy's mother is terminally ill and terribly poor, and Tammy goes to Jacksonville every month to help take care of her and manage her affairs. Financially, it's eating their lunch. They don't need any more expenses. Ted, their son, is great. I hope my boy turns out to have the character he does. But Ted has some learning difficulties, and Jeff and Tammy have to get special assistance for him. Jeff told me the other day that with all the changes in their circumstances, they may have to move into a less expensive neighborhood because they're being financially drained. On top of everything else, they've just found out their car is going to need major repairs. What I'm getting at is that he is one good guy who has known nothing but headaches and hardship. He never complains, but there is nobody who has more right to.

Now let's talk about the opposite end of our block. Ken, his wife, Michelle, and their self-centered daughter, Diane, are the kind of neighbors you would love to live without. Nobody in this neighborhood trusts them. If I drove past their house and my hubcap came off, Ken would probably try to grab it as it was spinning down the street. Then he'd take it to some junk dealer and make every nickel he could on it, and he's the last guy who needs money. It's no wonder he's filthy rich. He's grabbed every dollar he could from wherever he could get it. My hubcap example is obviously an exaggeration, but the point is, that family lives for three people only—themselves. On top of that, they are arrogant. Whenever you're around them, they give you the impression that they are too high and mighty to talk to you. As you well know, I'm not a praying man, but if our neighborhood has a block party, I pray they don't show up.

Rumors in this neighborhood travel fast. We heard last December that Ken's company might transfer him. Most of us were hopeful it would be to the other side of the country, or better yet, outside the U.S. That would have been the best Christmas present we could have received. If you get the impression they're an easy family to hate, you're right. And their language is disgusting. Sure, I let a few curse words slip, but I'm really convinced that four-letter words are all Ken and Michelle know.

Do you know what else? Everything goes right for Ken. He gives to nobody, takes from everybody, and never has anything negative happen to him. At work, he's in the million-dollar club—not because he's a hard worker, but because he's a smooth talker. Once he uses you for his own selfish advantage, he's gone. Three months ago, his boss rewarded him with a company car—a new Lexus. For the first two weeks he had it, he parked it outside the garage as much as possible so we'd all see it. I would have been thrilled if the big oak tree by their driveway had fallen across that car! It would have made a lot of us happy. He would have gotten what he deserved—probably for the first time in his life.

Sure, I know. There's more to life than money. There has to be. But nothing goes wrong for them. They've made it known that when Ken's father dies, they are going to get a big inheritance. They've even looked at a lake house they plan to buy with the money. I know this sounds crude, but I wouldn't be surprised if Ken tried to hasten his dad's death just to get that money sooner.

Do you see why I'm confused? I could give a lot more examples. It seems so often that the best people have things go wrong and they suffer constantly. The worst people have everything go right. They prosper. Most people wouldn't call me the best, although alongside Ken and his family, I look like a saint! Neither would they call me the worst. When I do a simple comparison, the luck of the bad guys is sure more inviting than the luck of the good guys. I'd rather be a bad guy.

Chuck

Looking at Chuck

Chuck has a "chip on his shoulder." Since he tends to be a decent, respectable human being, it bothers him that wicked people prosper and the righteous suffer. As justifiable as that concern is, it makes him overlook two things. These two things could serve as an opportunity for presenting the gospel to Chuck.

Chuck operates on a basic false presupposition: If God is not doing anything now, He is not going to do anything ever! Nothing could be further from the truth. If Chuck can come to see how God takes the long-range view of life, he'll discover that the wicked are not as "lucky" as he thinks they are. That may change his focus. He'll see that the emphasis is not what is happening at the moment but what is going to happen in the future. With that in mind, Chuck will have to concern himself, not with Jeff or Ken, but with Chuck.

The second mistake Chuck makes is that he sees everybody's sins but his own, primarily because he is a master of comparison. He looks terrible alongside Jeff but terribly good alongside Ken. He needs to see God as one who makes comparisons as well, but the only one God compares any of us to is Jesus Christ. Unless Chuck sees himself as God sees him—as a sinner—he'll never understand his need for Christ. He must be confronted with his sin and the substitutionary death and resurrection of Christ.

Chuck makes an interesting disclosure. He begins his letter to Carlton by saying, "I want to ask you about something that has bothered me off and on for years." But then it becomes obvious that he's jealous of Ken for being in the million-dollar club. Apparently, materialism has quite a hold on Chuck. Not only are "things" too important to Ken, they are also too important to Chuck. Instead of looking at what the wicked have and saying, "So what," Chuck says, "I wish." Again, a proper view of life, recognizing what is temporary and what is permanent, is needed to cure his distorted perspective on "things."

Responding to Chuck

Dear Chuck,

I wish more people would spell out what bothers them the way you do. If they would just talk it out, a lot of their confusion could be resolved.

I know you haven't had many meaningful experiences with religion, but the next time we get together, I want us to look in the Bible at a book called Psalms. I'm particularly thinking of chapter 37 of that book. I'll show you that God does identify with your struggles—far more than you think. There is a paragraph that says, "The wicked plots against the just, and gnashes at him with his teeth. The Lord laughs at him, for He sees that his day is coming. The wicked have drawn the sword and have bent their bow, to cast down the poor and needy, to slay those who are of upright conduct. Their sword shall enter their own heart, and their bows shall be broken."

One of the hardest things for people to understand is that God takes the long-range view of life. He knows about everything good that has happened to Ken and everything bad that Jeff has suffered, but He also knows their situations are temporary. Sixty, seventy, or eighty years from now, it will all be over. If Ken and his family don't come to Christ, God will have no choice but to punish them in eternal separation from Himself. Everything evil and selfish they've done will be brought back to them, and they will pay for their sins forever. What's more, when they see their sin from His perspective, they will know they're getting everything they deserve.

God's Son, Jesus Christ, was never a negative, pessimistic person. He didn't earn His reputation as a friend of sinners by being unloving. He was so loving that He often spoke directly, though compassionately, about hell. Hell, as He forewarned, is the worst punishment anyone can imagine. So, whenever you get irritated and frustrated, remember—the wicked are enjoying the fruits of their wickedness now, but when you contrast life on earth with eternity, you'll realize that their enjoyment is for a short period of time. They will discover that it would have been better to have God, and nothing else in this world, than seemingly having everything and yet not have Him.

Jesus Christ was a good communicator and often used stories to illustrate truth. When we look at the Bible, I'll show you something in the sixteenth chapter of Luke that will interest you. It describes two people who were as different in life as they were in death. After you've read it, you can then ask yourself the simple question, "Who fared the best?" I think you will begin to see what I mean about taking the long-range view of life.

Let me mention two more things that will be helpful to you. You made the kind of comment many people make. "Alongside Ken and his family, I look like a saint." I agree—from your perspective, you do. You are a decent and respectable person. But, Chuck, God doesn't compare anyone on earth with you or you with anyone else. Instead, He measures everyone by one standard—His Son, Jesus Christ, who was absolutely perfect. Alongside Him, everybody falls short. No, God doesn't like Ken's cursing, but neither does He enjoy my impatience with my wife. Remember, His standard is perfection. Every single person you've met or will meet is a sinner.

That's why Jesus died on the cross. God wanted to forgive you, not punish you. His holy nature demands that sin be punished. He can't make excuses for sin or lower His standard. I once saw a billboard that had a cross on it and the words, It was for you. That's what the Bible is saying, Chuck. The punishment for sin is death. Jesus, God's perfect Son, took your punishment on a cross. He suffered in our place as our substitute. When He died on the cross, it was for you and me. Because He died for our sins and rose on the third day, He can now forgive us for all our sins. You can receive that forgiveness by trusting Christ as your personal Savior. I so want you to do that. Otherwise, you've left Him no choice but to make you pay for your own sins, just as Ken is going to have to pay for his if he doesn't come to Christ.

When you think about it, God has done a lot in your life to let you know He cares for you. Have you ever had to worry about your next meal? That fender bender you told me about the other day could have been a lot worse. As people often say, "Somebody upstairs must have been watching over you." But nothing explains more how He cares for you than that event two thousand years ago when He died for you.

This is the second thing I want to mention. Perhaps the next time I see you we can spend more time on it. Remember what I said about taking the long-range view of life? The wicked have a day coming when they will receive their due punishment, but don't forget that those who do right will also have their due.

Doing good things doesn't get anyone to heaven. There are many good people who will not go to heaven because they are trusting their own goodness instead of God's Son to save them. I want to keep emphasizing that forgiveness and the gift of life eternal are free. At the same time, once a person trusts Christ to save him and lives in a way that demonstrates gratitude for the gift of eternal life, that person will have his reward. All those who have trusted Christ as Savior will be in heaven, but they won't all be equally rewarded. That's why, in the last book of the Bible, God declares, "Behold, I am coming quickly, and My reward is with Me, to give to every one according to his work." Wait until Jeff and Tammy see what God has waiting for them. I'm sure they have no regrets now that they are living for Christ, and I promise you they won't when they get to heaven. They will be abundantly rewarded.

You see, in that way God is both loving and fair. He is loving because "whosoever," as the Bible repeatedly says, can come to Him. But He's fair. If a person comes to Christ at an early age and then lives for Him, he has a whole lifetime to accumulate rewards—something that a person who comes to Christ on his deathbed doesn't have.

When you see things from the perspective I'm talking about, everything looks very different. Many people might feel that your neighbor Jeff could not be doing worse and Ken could not be doing better. But the fact is, if we look at things from eternity backward, Jeff could not be doing any better and Ken could not be doing any worse. In a sentence, Jeff is living for what does matter and Ken is living for what doesn't matter.

Chuck, there are many times when I'd like to have more, materially speaking. I wish we didn't have to watch our budget the way we do. But then I start thinking, "What's all that going to matter one hundred years from now?" And I realize that whatever priorities I have now will be the same ones my two boys will have. Wow, then I really start to think.

Please consider coming to Christ. He'll gladly do for you what He did for me: forgive you for all the wrongs you've done and give you the gift of eternal life. Your family loves and respects you. I know if you accept Christ they'll probably follow. They know how well you think things through. Once you have

Christ in your life, you'll find it difficult not to tell them what's happened. If you simply live for Christ, you won't regret it. Regardless of what happens on earth, He's keeping the books. No good deed will go unrewarded. He's promised that.

I'm praying for you, Chuck. You know how much I respect and appreciate you.

Carlton

Alex's Struggle

Please bear with me.
I take all this religion stuff very seri-
ously and plan to become a Christian,
but first I want to have some fun in life.

Who Is Alex?

A twenty-five-year-old in the party haven of Las Vegas, Alex has one thing on his mind: the next party. Although he would deny it, he takes the message of Christianity and the matter of his own sinfulness quite lightly. With a good job, plenty of money, and many friends to hang around with, he has no interest in being bored with the Christian life.

Listening to Alex

Dear Darrell,

I would hope that God, with his stature, is not easily threatened. After all, he's got it all—power, position, intelligence, the whole works—and I don't mean that facetiously. When I've read the Bible, I've found parts of it that scare me. God strikes me as someone who doesn't mess around. I sort of believe what you explained to me about God's Son being the only way to eternal life, so I plan to come to him. I'm no fool. Only a fool would want to go to hell.

But I'll be honest. First, I want to have some fun. I'm the party guy—eat, drink, and be merry. I live for the weekends, no use denying it. I have done some things that are pretty bad, but somehow, I never get caught. I'm the kind of guy who gets away with just about everything. I know something could catch up with me, but I doubt it. I'm going strong at twenty-five and don't plan to slow down right now.

Later on I am going to become a Christian. I've promised myself that. Like I've said, only a fool would want to go to hell. In fact, if there is anything I could do that would exclude me from his kingdom, please tell me. It's kind of like the question I saw on a T-shirt: "How much can I get away with and still go to heaven?" I wish I knew where the guy got it. I'd like to have one. I need to know, though. I certainly don't want to do anything that would mess up my chances.

I'm not saying God isn't exciting, but, like I told you, most of the Christians I know aren't as much fun to be around as the rest of my friends. In fact, some of them are kind of long faced. Please don't be offended, Darrell. I'm not including you, although quite frankly your life does seem rather boring compared to mine. Let me have some fun and then let's talk again. Kind of put me on your "later" list. Fair enough?

Alex

Looking at Alex

Alex is the type of person with whom you cut to the chase. Because he is direct, he opens himself up for the believer to be direct with him.

Being direct shouldn't mean being insulting. Alex, in many respects, has a warped mind and a warped conscience, so he can say some things that do seem a bit insulting. Getting annoyed with him would do little good and perhaps much harm. He's only reflecting his condition. He's blinded by Satan and controlled by his sinful nature.

Alex doesn't face reality. We all know that tomorrow could

be his last. Facing non-Christians with the reality of death can be very effective. But trying to get Alex alarmed about this reality would probably do little good since he feels he is the great escape artist. It would be far more effective to try correcting his distorted definition of what a party is and help him see how unlikely it is that, if he keeps putting it off, he'll ever come to Christ. That way, every passing day might move him to reflect on the questions, "How serious am I about coming to Christ? If it doesn't happen soon, will it ever happen?"

Alex should excite any believer who has the kind of relationship with him Darrell does. Alex is not the type to say, "I respect and appreciate you," but the fact that he is comfortable being candid with Darrell proves he does. God has amazing ways of getting the attention of people like Alex. Perhaps He might even put him on his back one day as he's traveling the fast lane and make him look up. If Alex will listen to anyone at that time, it would no doubt be Darrell.

Alex has to see sin for what it is and see himself for who he is: a sinner condemned by God. The danger to be avoided, though, is a "you-versus-me" mentality in which he thinks you're saying, "You're a sinner, but I'm not." Bringing yourself into the conversation, your own rebellion against God and the background from which you were saved, could mean a lot to Alex when he reflects on it. And Alex will reflect on it. The Spirit of God will see to that. There will undoubtedly be nights when God and Alex are alone, and he'll think over Darrell's words.

Responding to Alex

Dear Alex,

You're right. You are the party guy! You rarely miss an opportunity for a grand time. When you decide to do something, you go all the way. And I don't doubt that your plans to come to Christ are sincere.

Alex, our candid relationship means a lot to me, so I can say up front that there are some things about your life that frighten me. Once I explain myself, you might decide that you're not having as much fun as you think you are.

I commend you for your sincerity, but that doesn't mean you always face facts. Your idea of fun is women, parties, alcohol, and anything else that leaves you feeling guilty! That's right—guilty. How do I know that? It's the expression you have on your face when you talk about what you've done, and when you say, "I know I probably shouldn't have, but . . ." If being a "party guy" is so much fun, why do you feel guilty? Have you ever admitted to yourself that you often go to the next party trying to get the last party off your mind? Your guilty feelings are understandable. God has given each of us a conscience. When we do something wrong, no one needs to tell us. Our consciences do that. Sometimes we feel so unclean that we try to ignore our consciences. That doesn't really work, but we keep trying. Is that really fun? Or let me put it another way. Why does your laughter seem to stop the same time the party does?

Talking about facing facts, you made a comment I find interesting. Your words were, "Most of the Christians I know aren't as much fun to be around as the rest of my friends." Come on, Alex! I'm aware of three Christians you know, and I'm one of them. I seriously doubt you've spent more than thirty minutes with any of us. One of them invited you to go to a college football game two months ago with his friends. You told me you turned him down because you were afraid he would talk to you about the Lord. You're right! He probably would have. Sam has been a "tiger" for the Lord ever since he came to Christ. He's lost some friends over it, but at least they know where he stands. How do you know what these Christian friends are really like when you've never spent much time with them? Give them a chance, and don't form any opinions until you do. You'd get upset if somebody prejudged you. Don't they have the same right? Maybe we're not as long faced as you think.

Do you realize that none of your parties last more than a few hours? God offers a party that will last forever. Yes—forever! In the Bible God doesn't say a lot about what heaven is like, probably because if He did we couldn't comprehend it. When those who come to Christ arrive in heaven, they are going to experience something so far beyond anything they've ever seen, it's unimaginable. Best of all, it's never going to end! It will start and never stop. Now that's a party!

I care what happens to you, Alex, I just want you to wake up before it's too late. Do me a favor. Take a sheet of paper and draw a line down the middle of that sheet. On the left side of the line put all the characteristics of one of your parties. Don't leave anything out. I'll get you started: drinking, friends, music, laughter, women, dancing, jokes, and, occasionally, drugs. Add anything else that I have not mentioned. You've been straightforward with me. Now be honest with yourself.

Then, on the right side of that paper, list all the characteristics of God's party. Since you don't know what they are, I'll tell you some (and I could show you all of these in the Bible): happiness, peace of mind, contentment, reason for living, love for others, self-control, forgiveness, no guilt, and, once more, eternal life. Then, back off and look at the two columns. If you choose the left one over the right, I care enough to say, "You are a fool." Don't be a fool, Alex.

You're twenty-five, and you mentioned that you seem to escape everything. You're right about that. Most people with your lifestyle would be dead by your age. But you always seem to know where and when to stop. You're probably expecting me to say that something tragic is about to happen. None of us knows how long we're going to live, but I wouldn't be surprised if you lived to be eighty. The Lord could tell you definitely how many days you have. In the Bible, there's a book called Job. Referring to the fact that God knows the amount of time we have, chapter 14, verse 5 says, "Since his days are determined, the number of his months is with You; You have appointed his limits, so that he cannot pass." But what you don't know is that the longer you delay, the harder it's going to be for you to come to Christ. Even now, you probably look back on your list of accomplishments and feel as though you don't need Him. That feeling will intensify—not diminish. It is difficult for you to humble yourself now. Think what it is going to be like fifty to sixty years from now! Your pride will be so great, and your stubbornness will be so strong, that even knowing the day's approaching when you're going to meet God face to face won't shake you up that much. One reason for that is that Satan has done a great job of blinding you to your real need. He will do his best to keep you that way—totally blind to how much you need Jesus—now, as well as fifty years from now. If you knew statistically how few people came to Christ after age forty, it would scare you.

One more thing. You asked me if there was anything that would jeopardize your chances of going to heaven. In terms of a particular sin, the answer is no. There is nothing that could keep you out of heaven because there is no sin God can't forgive. When Jesus Christ died for you on the cross and rose on the third day, He paid the price for every sin. God will forgive you and give you life eternal the moment you trust His Son as your Savior. But before you can come to Him, you have to see sin for what it is. Since He is a holy God, sin is sin. The only choice He has is to punish you for it. Confess what deep down in your conscience you know—you are a sinner—and let God forgive you. If He could forgive me, Alex, He certainly can forgive you, or, for that matter, anybody. You know where I used to be. There are many times I've wished I had back the money and the years I spent on alcohol and drugs.

I promise you one thing, or to say it more accurately, God promises you one thing. If you come to Christ, He will introduce you to a real party. Remember what your own high school buddy, who came to Christ a month ago, told you. In the ten minutes you had to talk with him, you noticed that he was the happiest you'd ever seen him. You told me his comment to you was, "Coming to Christ has meant everything. This is the happiest I've ever been." Remember that? By the way, why didn't you include him in the list of Christians you know?

I hope I haven't lost your friendship by expressing my thoughts. I wouldn't want that to happen, but the risk is worth it. Your address five seconds after you die means even more to me than our friendship. Please, Alex, think really hard about all this. Wouldn't you agree that a lot of it makes sense?

Darrell

Nathan's Struggle

I've listened to many people talk about God, but they all have different opinions about how a person comes to him. Why?

Who Is Nathan?

Nathan is in Confusion with a capital "C." He has grown up in the Bible belt of Tennessee, where he's employed by a sales company. Many people have approached him about his need for Christ. Not a deep thinker, he listens to what others say without weighing things very heavily. He has no struggle accepting the reality of God, and he's never doubted that the Bible is a book God wrote. He's quite ready to recognize his need and come to Christ. He's simply trying to sort out everything he's heard.

Listening to Nathan

Dear Jack,

I was not disturbed at all that you asked me about my relationship with God the other day. You aren't the first person to do so. My mother-in-law hounds me almost every week. At least you didn't turn me off the way she does. I'm not sure why. But let me explain something that bothers me.

I would be thrilled if even two Christians could get their stories straight. Whenever any of them have talked to me about God, or I should say, have tried to stuff God down my throat, no two of them have said the same thing. It's no secret that I smoke. One of them told me that if I wanted to come to God I'd have to give up smoking. The fact that I've gone from two packs to one pack a day didn't particularly impress him, and I take it from what he said it doesn't particularly impress God, either. God sounds a lot like my wife. She nags me constantly about the money I put into cigarettes—money she has a hundred and one other uses for. I've tried kicking the habit, and I can't. Everybody's got to go some time, and I figure my way might as well be emphysema or lung cancer.

Then another Christian told me that God requires I be baptized. For me that's scary. I love swimming, but going to the front of the church and getting water poured over me or getting dunked by someone who's wearing a white evening gown isn't exactly swimming to me. At least that is the way I've always pictured it. I don't know what this baptizing thing is, and I don't even think the fellow who suggested it knows. If he does, he sure didn't do a very good job of explaining it.

Then there's Lisa, my secretary at work. She has another version. I had lunch one day with a business associate who confronted me about my language. He said he didn't appreciate the way I used God's name. I was shocked! A lot of Christians strike me as being wimps who are afraid to tell you what they think. But he didn't mess around. When I came back from lunch, I told my secretary what had happened. She's never mentioned God or the Bible to me. She then told me she was a Christian. And guess what? She also informed me that I had to be part of her church to be what she called "saved." To hear her speak, God has this elite group that she's in, but most of the world isn't. I'm glad she hasn't conveyed that attitude in business, or I guarantee you, she wouldn't be going on her eighth year with me.

What about it, Jack? If you spoke to five Christians, they'd all have a different way to God. How do I know who is right? They all seem to claim some Bible verse for their position.

I probably have no right to criticize God, but you know what I often think? I earn my living in sales. When we train salespeople, we teach them all to say the same thing. If you spoke to any two members of my sales force, they might use different words and reflect their own personalities, but they'd all tell you the same facts and give you the same figures. I wonder if something has broken down in the "training" Christians are given. Even if I ended up rejecting the whole thing, it would be comforting to have two people give the same story about how a person gets from where I am to where God is.

Don't I have a right to be confused? Aren't most people? Try to be objective, Jack, and I think you'll agree that I have a good point.

Nathan

Looking at Nathan

The book of the Bible that unbelievers must be directed to is the fourth book of the New Testament: John. Many believers are not aware that it is the book written for non-Christians. John acknowledges that as God's purpose when he says in John 20:31, "But these are written that you may believe that Jesus is the Christ, the Son of God, and that believing you may have life in His name." When we take an unbeliever to the gospel of John, the focus is no longer what one person or another says but what God says. The thrilling thing about the book is that, although there are parts of the Bible that are hard to understand, the gospel of John is not one of them. If we study it with an open mind, we cannot misunderstand the message. Ninety-eight times God uses the word believe in this book that He wrote for non-Christians.

When non-Christians mention negative issues such as the fanaticism of believers, we have a great opportunity to present the gospel. Instead of being defensive, we can simply apologize for any improper way others have conducted themselves and encourage the non-Christian by saying, "Don't get so annoyed with the messenger that you miss the message." Then we can clearly explain the good news of Christ's death and resurrection.

Non-Christians, at times, get distracted by baptism. Someone faithful to the Scriptures cannot say, "Don't worry about it. You don't ever have to be baptized." God does command it of those who desire to grow as His disciples. The Great Commission tells us, "Go therefore and make disciples of all the nations, baptizing them in the name of the Father and of the Son and of the Holy Spirit" (Matt. 28:19). Any discussion of baptism, though, can become an opportunity for presenting the gospel if we make two things clear to the non-Christian: (1) the biblical place of baptism is after we come to Christ, and (2) that we often want to be baptized after becoming a Christian because of what Christ has done for us. This affords a way of saying to non-Christians, "You are missing out on two things: a free gift and the genuine excitement of having Christ indwell your life. These things can make everything you do a response of gratitude."

When an unbeliever struggles with certain habits, he sometimes feels so overwhelmed and controlled by them that the difficulty is not whether he wants to stop. Nathan's words certainly indicate that he wishes he had never started smoking. Instead, he wonders if he can quit. For the sake of the lost, it is helpful to mention people in worse situations, humanly speaking, whom God has transformed. This puts the stress on the non-believer's need of the Savior. It also offers another thing that non-Christians need: hope (even though some of them are more conscious of it than others). This is a good time to bring in the details of one's own testimony or the testimony of others.

Responding to Nathan

Dear Nathan,

There's no use denying it. I wouldn't even try. You're not alone. A lot of people who ponder God at times, as you have, experience the same thing you have. You're astute in recognizing that all "Christians" are not saying the same thing.

Nathan, there are parts of the Bible that people find difficult to understand. But there are parts of it that cannot be misunderstood. For example, the fourth book of the New Testament is a book called John, and it's the book God wrote for non-Christians. The purpose of that book is declared in the twentieth chapter and the thirty-first verse: "But these are written that you may believe that Jesus is the Christ, the Son of God, and that believing you may have life in His name." Please, Nathan, do me a favor, for your sake more than anyone's. Take time out from your job to sit down and read that book from beginning to end. Stop listening to what everybody else is saying—including me—and examine the facts for yourself. You have a good mind. That's one reason you've done so well in business. Read the book of John for yourself, and find out what God says about how to come to Him.

If you read the book of John, you'll discover that one word is used over and over. It's the word believe. It means to depend on, to trust. For example, one verse you will find in the first part of that book simply says, "He who believes in Me has everlasting life." It's the forty-seventh verse of chapter six. That verse isn't hard to understand. If a person comes to God as a sinner and trusts Christ as his only way to heaven, God will give him, completely free, the gift of eternal life. If you read the gospel of John, you will discover that He emphasizes that same thing many, many times.

This free gift surprises a lot of people. Why would He do that? Because His perfect Son has already taken the punishment for your sins. The punishment you deserve He has taken, and He did it for only one reason—because He loves you.

Do you remember a few weeks ago I was telling you about

Eric, our five-year-old? He's never met a stranger. Give him about twenty more years, and he'll probably be able to take over your sales company. Well, last night he got into a heap of trouble. After dinner, Elizabeth and I looked out the window and saw him taking candy from a stranger parked on the side of the road. I've never been more terrified in my life. I opened the front door just as Eric was about to open the car door. When the driver saw me, he sped off. Eric didn't walk back to the house. He was whisked there by my arm and my anger! I had to discipline him more severely than he's ever been disciplined before. But I knew it was necessary. He had disobeyed me. I don't know how many times we have told him not to speak to strangers. Eric didn't see what happened next, though. I walked into our bedroom after sending him to his room and broke down. I was all torn up inside. I had never been so angry, and I was overwhelmed by what could have happened. On the one hand, I could have lost the son I love; on the other hand, I had had to punish him severely—something that is hard for me to do in any circumstances. I kept telling Elizabeth, "I hope he knows I'm doing this because I love him."

Nathan, God loves you, too, but because you have disobeyed Him, your sin must be punished. Instead of punishing you, however, He allowed His Son, Jesus Christ, to die in your place on a cross. The harsh and cruel death that you should have suffered, He suffered for you. He was your substitute. He willingly died in your place. When He rose on the third day, it was proof that He had taken on Himself the punishment for sin and had conquered both sin and death. For that reason, God can now extend eternal life to any who will trust His Son Jesus Christ as their only way to heaven.

In the book of John, God never talks about coming to church. Check it out, and you'll see it's true. He only talks about coming to Christ. If you trust Him as your Savior, going to church would become a very meaningful experience. You'd be worshiping with other people who know Him. They'd encourage you, and you'd encourage them. We'd love to have you come with us. But that's not what concerns me at the moment. Going to church does not make anyone a Christian, and neither do baptism, living a good life, keeping the commandments, taking the sacraments, and some of the other things you've heard. Going to church is important. If you come to Christ, the people there would help you learn more about Him. But church attendance has nothing to do with your eternal destiny.

I know what you're asking, "Then why do people tell me different and wrong things?" Because, Nathan, God's enemy is Satan. He does his absolute best to keep people from coming to Christ. One way he works his deceit is through those you're calling "Christians." Some of the ones you've called Christians are not actually His children—for the simple reason that they are depending on their good works, church membership, or baptism to get them to heaven instead of Christ. God made it clear in the Bible that some of the most religious people will never see heaven because they've not trusted Christ to save them. Instead, they are relying on their own good works and religious efforts. When you study the book of John, you'll notice that Jesus Christ had a much harder time reaching the religious zealots than He did reaching the people called "sinners" in the town. God wants those who have been deceived to come to Him. However, instead of reading what His book says about how to come to Him, as I've encouraged you to do, people come up with their own ideas. Please read the book of John. You'll find out how many, many times God has said there that if a person simply believes in Christ he'll have everlasting life.

I need to explain something to you. There are many who are genuine Christians, but in their eagerness they don't always speak clearly. They know there is only one way to God: personal trust in Christ. But in their excitement, they forget how confused they were when they were in your shoes. They have reason to be enthusiastic. As you can tell, I'm enthusiastic, too. In fact, when we finished talking the other day, I was hoping my own excitement about Christ didn't bother you. But I can't help it. I've found in Christ the number one thing in life: absolute certainty that when I die I'll go to heaven.

Besides that, I've found a happiness I have never known and a reason to look forward to Monday as much as I do to Friday. I don't live for the weekends the way I used to. Sometimes the excitement of Christians gets ahead of their clarity and patience with others. I know you've been annoyed by the way some Christians have "stuffed" Jesus down your throat, but please understand where they are coming from. They mean well even if they don't have a lot of tact.

You mentioned your smoking. No, you don't have to give it up to come to Christ. God never said that. Believe me, Nathan, people have come to Christ with a lot more against them than you have. In many cases their lives were a mess. Even they called them that. But that's how God wants people to come to Him—mess and all. Speaking of messes, Elizabeth has a nephew who is currently in prison for capital murder. He and two other people were involved in the killing of a police officer. Her nephew wasn't the trigger man, but he was in the car with the fellow who was. After several months in prison, he came to Christ, and is he ever growing. Even the guards have noticed the change. Most people wouldn't view anything we've done as even close to the magnitude of what he was involved in. But the God who accepted him just as he was—a mess—also accepted me. And He'll accept you, too. In one way or another, small or great, we all make a mess of our lives without Christ.

If you trust His Son as the Savior who died for you on the cross and rose again, God will give you the free gift of life eternal. Then, as you allow Him to, He'll send the Holy Spirit to work in your life. He'll help you, month by month, take out of your life what should not be there and put in what should. I really believe that, with Christ, you'd find the strength to give up smoking. It may not be easy, because physically you have gotten your body dependent on nicotine. But He's helped others, and He doesn't play favorites. He could help you, too. And once you come to Christ and see Him working in your life, you will probably be more patient with those people you call "fanatics." Why? Because you'll be excited to know you have the certainty of life forever with God, and you'll experience firsthand, even in bad months when sales are down, the peace and tranquillity you've never known. With Christ, even bad days become tolerable.

In fact, I'm thinking how appreciative you are of everything Lisa has done for you and the company. The best thing you could do for her is to come to Christ, and then explain the simple message from the book of John to her. God loves Lisa, but it sounds as though she's done what many people do. She's listened to what her church has said instead of reading what the Bible says. She's religious, but if she meant what she told you, she really doesn't know Christ as her Savior. Instead, she's depending, as so many do, on her decent behavior and church attendance to save her. If Lisa's good works could get her to heaven, God would never have had to die for her. I wish she'd do what I have encouraged you to do: read the book of John.

Let me explain baptism. Christ wasn't the one who originated it. Baptism was practiced many years before He walked the earth. It was simply a means by which people identified themselves with a particular message or messenger. It was a sign of identification. God asks those who trust Christ as their Savior to be baptized as a public declaration that they have come to Christ and now wish to follow Him. It's the first step of discipleship—following after Christ. Since Jesus was not ashamed to die for us on a cross, He certainly can ask us not to be ashamed of Him. I assure you, though, that baptism will not save anyone. That's why it is never mentioned in the gospel of John as a requirement for salvation. You will find that once you come to Christ, being baptized could be a very satisfying experience for you and it would also honor God. You would be telling people in no uncertain terms that He is yours and you are His. You would be saying publicly, "I've trusted Christ as my Savior and want to follow Him all my life." Your first concern has to be trusting Christ, though, not being baptized.

Once again, Nathan, study the book of John in the Bible. Sometimes the message of how a person gets from earth to heaven is so easy that people miss it. No one else would have made the way to heaven as simple as God made it. But then, no one else loves us the way He does, either.

He sure does want you to come to Him. And so do Elizabeth and I.

Jack

Greg's Struggle

*Jesus Christ was not the only one who
claimed to be God. Isn't it possible that he
was really just some guy on an ego trip?*

Who Is Greg?

Greg is an engineer, married with no children, who lives
in Los Angeles, California. An "up-and-rising" man in his company, he prides himself on being an intellectual who wants to
have all the facts before making a decision. Raised in a home
with an abusive father, he respects men who are kind instead
of abusive, but he is also very distrustful of them. His experience has proven to him that people are often a far cry from
who they claim to be.

Listening to Greg

Dear John,

I know you probably think I have a lot of nerve to say this,
but quite frankly, I don't think you always face reality. I don't
blame you for the way you feel about Jesus. I, too, think he was
a great person. In fact, from what I can tell, his teachings have
done more to change people than anyone else's. Look at what
he said about turning the other cheek, loving your neighbor,

and treating others the way you want them to treat you. If there were more people like Jesus around, the world would be a phenomenal place instead of the selfish mess it is now.

But it wasn't just what he said, it was how he said it. Years ago somebody told me that little kids used to want to sit on Jesus' lap. He strikes me as someone you would want as a father. As I've told you, John, I know I sure could have used him. My dad was the complete opposite. I couldn't wait to get out from under his roof. In fact, a few years ago when my mom and dad celebrated their fortieth wedding anniversary, all of us would have preferred it if Dad were not there. We've had all the screaming and yelling we can take from him, not to mention his self-centered demands. I'll guarantee you, if it weren't for Mom's believing how absolutely wrong divorce is, she wouldn't have stuck with him.

But anyway, back to Jesus. I'd call him a good man and a great teacher, but don't you think calling him "God" is stretching it a bit? Certainly you're aware he's not the only one who has made that claim. In fact, I've heard that many people have walked the earth claiming to be God. Maybe Jesus was sincere in thinking he was God, but let's face it, anyone can be sincerely wrong.

Look what occurred in Waco, Texas. That guy David Koresh created havoc. I've heard conflicting reports. One person told me David Koresh claimed to be Jesus. Another person told me he simply claimed to be sent by God. Anyway, when agents of the Bureau of Alcohol, Tobacco, and Firearms tried to raid his sect's compound, they weren't prepared for what they met. The sect members were well armed. As a result, four of the ATF agents and a number of sect members were killed. The standoff went on for months and ended tragically with the death of Koresh and many of his followers. I have an uncle in Texas who hates religion. He sent me an article from the Dallas Morning News that said something significant. I think he kept it just to prove his point to others. I have the article in front of me. It was the March 7, 1993, paper. It states, "America's rich religious heritage includes an array of beliefs. Some devout Catholics resolutely claim seeing a weeping Virgin Mary. A woman in a Midwestern town cites being healed of cancer in her living room after watching a television evangelist. All may say they have heard, seen, or been touched by God or some ethereal religious figure."

You get my point? Seems like anyone can get a group of people to follow him. Jesus had his act together. Maybe his followers were so excited about him that they elevated him into something he never was. He, too, may have been just a guy on an ego trip. Who isn't? I like attention myself. Guess what? I think I'm about to receive an award from my company for outstanding performance. If I do, it'll be presented to me at a dinner where about five hundred will attend. Am I looking forward to it? You betcha. I can't wait. All of us have an ego.

You know how much traveling I do. I've just come back from India. Our company is working on a major project in New Delhi, and four of us were assigned to it. I'll tell you more about it when we have lunch together again. I think it was my "prepromotion" trip. I wouldn't be surprised if my boss called me in tomorrow with some good news for me. Talk about religion. India is saturated with it. But from what I could observe over there, Hinduism, not Christianity, reigns supreme. They respect Jesus a lot. Somebody there told me that you've never experienced Christmas until you've experienced it in India. It's quite a holiday—the birthday of a great teacher, Jesus Christ. Other people and even objects are worshiped as God, but not Jesus. If you were to flip a coin, don't you think they have as much a right as anyone to the title? I like the way a person in this Dallas Morning News article put it: "One man's cult is another man's church."

I don't see that it makes a difference anyway. Whatever a person believes is just fine. Honestly, John, I think you should back off any insistence that Jesus is God. The bottom line is, it doesn't matter. Since there are a lot of other contenders for the position, isn't it sort of hopeless to try to prove that Jesus has a corner on the market?

Greg

Looking at Greg

Greg is an engineer. He deals with facts, not theories. That is excellent because the truth about the resurrection of Christ is built on just that—facts, not theories. Whatever John does, he should not deny these facts. They are true. Greg has an excellent point. Many people have walked the surface of the earth claiming to be God. To deny that would be to deny the evidence and to be less than truthful with non-Christians.

Non-Christians often do something that, in other areas, all of us do: They make a statement they haven't given serious thought to. Greg wrote, "It doesn't matter what you believe." Daily living, however, proves that sentiment is not valid. If it were, why would anyone want to know how "safe" something is before they use it or ride in it? This reality becomes a very helpful starting point to get a non-Christian thinking.

The issues with which Greg must be confronted are the cross and the empty tomb. The cross removes all doubt that Christ was on an ego trip. People on ego trips don't die for the wrongs of others. The empty tomb is one of the best documented facts of history. It is almost certain that Greg has never thought about spiritual things from this angle.

Greg is doing exactly the opposite of what occurs in real life. In real life, at a trial, the accused party is innocent until proven guilty, not guilty until proven innocent. Since Greg appears to be sincere, he can probably be shown that Christ deserves a verdict of innocent until proven otherwise.

It is a well-known fact that many, if not most, of us receive our impression of God from our experiences with our earthly fathers. Fortunately, Greg has not let this happen. That becomes an excellent opportunity to commend him, and, in so doing, to tear down any defensive feelings he might have. As I keep emphasizing, compliments play a big part in letting people know we appreciate them, even though some of their thinking is wrong. Applauding a non-Christian when he is thinking correctly lays a foundation for us to set him right when he begins to think incorrectly.

Responding to Greg

Dear Greg,

I like the way you are completely honest about your thoughts. The best way to express what I want to share is to say, "You could not be any more right and any more wrong."

You're right in saying that many others have walked the earth claiming to be God. To use your words, Jesus Christ does not have a "corner on the market" for claims of deity.

But, Greg, think about it. It does matter what you believe. Faith is no better than the object on which it rests. If you have faith that your car can travel on water, does it matter if it can't? It certainly does. It doesn't matter how sincere you are or how strong your faith is, cars don't travel on water.

I know what you saw while you were in India. I've never been there, but you know how much I like to read, and I've read a lot about that country. The next time we have lunch, I'd love to have you fill me in about the trip. Congratulations on being one of the four people chosen to go. In addition to meeting Hindus, I'm sure you met those who claimed allegiance to Muhammad. His followers, too, are very widespread. The next time you're there, politely ask them to show you Muhammad's empty tomb. Why? It doesn't exist. That, Greg, is the thing that sets Jesus Christ apart from all the others who claimed deity. Christ didn't stay in the grave. Three days after His death, He rose from it.

You have an open mind, and you are always willing to learn. That is one of the many things I respect you for. I encourage you to study the historical evidence behind the empty tomb of Christ. I have a book or two I would be happy to loan you in which people who have studied the historical evidence of Christ document their findings. I promise you will discover that the empty tomb of Christ is one of the best documented facts in history. You would be hard pressed to find an event in history with greater support than the resurrection of Jesus Christ.

So why are there so many impostors? It's because of something you don't know about. As far as I can remember, we've never talked about it. God has an enemy. His name is Satan. He will try to convince people to follow another "messiah" without questioning that person's claim. That way, he can lead millions of people down the wrong road and, ultimately, to hell. Some religions emphasize people's feelings and emotions. Those feelings aren't enough. There must be factual evidence to substantiate the feelings. Remember my example of the car traveling on water? If the facts are wrong, the feelings don't matter. Everything about Jesus Christ is based on fact. His resurrection on the third day proves that He is the One He claimed to be. Are you aware that nobody has ever disproved the resurrection? Even skeptics and those who never accepted Christ's message have admitted that the one thing they could not disprove was His resurrection.

Think about it. If Jesus Christ did not rise on the third day, why didn't His enemies simply produce the body? A large stone was rolled across the entrance to Christ's tomb, and the Roman guards watched that stone day and night to ensure that the body was not stolen. His enemies didn't produce the body because they didn't have it! He had supernaturally risen.

I know your schedule is full, but take time out as soon as you can and go back into history to find out for yourself what others have said about it. You won't regret it.

I just finished serving jury duty. The court kept reminding us that a person is innocent until proven guilty. It dawned on me during the trial that when I heard George Washington was the first president of the United States, I accepted that without question—even though I'd never spoken to anyone who saw him or heard him. Why don't you give Jesus Christ the same chance? Don't pronounce Him guilty of being a hoax until you've checked it out for yourself.

There is something else that's extremely important. You mentioned that Christ was a great teacher. You've overlooked the fact, though, that if He was not God, He was not a great teacher. Instead, Greg, He was a liar. Why? Because He never claimed to be a great teacher; He claimed He was God and allowed others to recognize and worship Him as such. To have represented Himself as God if, in fact, He was not, would make Him a deceitful teacher and, again, a liar.

You mentioned the other day that you have a Bible at home that your parents gave you years ago. Take that Bible and turn to the fourteenth chapter of the gospel of John. Notice how many times Jesus says that He and God are one and the same. Then turn to the twentieth chapter of the same book. When Jesus Christ arose from the grave and appeared before crowds of people, Thomas, one of the original twelve disciples, acclaimed Him, "My Lord and my God." For Christ to have accepted that kind of worship and not be God would have been the depth of deception.

There is no other option, Greg. Was Jesus God or wasn't He? If He wasn't, He was the greatest impostor there ever was.

You brought up the bad experiences you've had with your dad. I can't believe the way your dad treated you and the rest of your family. Fortunately, you haven't let that affect your feelings toward God the way so many others do. People have a way of transferring their feelings about their human father to God as a heavenly Father. If their human father was a real grouch, they assume God's the same. If they could only look beyond this transference, they'd find out that nobody has ever loved them the way God does.

Nothing you said concerns me more than when you mentioned the possibility of Jesus Christ being just a guy on an ego trip. People on ego trips don't die on a cross for others. People wear crosses around their necks like gold medals. They mean well, but you must keep in mind that the cross Christ died on was not an honor. Crucifixion was the way they put to death the most wicked criminals. I assure you, Christ's death came slowly and painfully. He easily could have escaped such a death. God could have snatched Him away, or He could have snatched Himself away. Instead, He died on that cross—a cross that was an object of humiliation and shame. The cross was most certainly not part of an ego trip.

Why did He die? Because of something I think you still don't understand. Look around your house a minute. Everything you have and own you've worked hard for. And you are a hard worker! Because of that, your feelings are the same as most people. You think that to get to heaven you have to work your way there. You don't understand. Jesus Christ has already paid for all you've done wrong. That's what His death on the cross is all about. He suffered the punishment for everything wrong you have ever done. He actually died for you and me—in our place. That's why He can now forgive you. Your punishment has already been taken by another—God's perfect Son. His resurrection on the third day is proof that He has conquered sin and death.

All you need to do is come to God as a sinner, and put your trust in His Son to forgive your sins and give you the free gift of eternal life . Notice I said "free gift." That's what eternal life is—a free gift to the person who will trust God's Son as his only way to heaven.

Please, Greg, keep thinking and studying. I want you to find in Christ the same thing I've found. I know I'm going to heaven when I die, and life with Christ right now has a happiness and purpose I've never known before. I respect our friendship, and I want this assurance and purpose for you, too.

Let's keep talking. Your interest and thoughts mean a lot to me.

John

Brian's Struggle

If God is as loving as he claims to be,
how in the world can he send
anyone to hell?

Who Is Brian?

Brian and his family live in Minnesota where he just recently got a job in real estate. His wife, Joanne, became pregnant while they were dating and had an abortion. Now, married two years with one son less than a year old, things are starting to come together for him, and he's starting to make something of his life. His conscience tells him that some things he's done wrong are just that—wrong. But he can't change the past. The fact that God would punish him for things he's done haunts him at times. But Brian can't conceive of a loving God sending someone to hell, especially since he is doing some things right.

Listening to Brian

Dear Blake,

If I've heard it once, I've heard it a thousand times—God loves us. You must be the umpteenth person I've heard say it.

That's precisely where I'm struggling. Is it true? If God is as loving as he claims to be, how can he send anyone to hell?

I'm not one to complain, but that is the biggest contradiction I've ever heard. For quite some time now I've heard preachers talk about love and forgiveness. Then they turn around and talk about hell. Even the way they talk about it upsets me. Sometimes they seem excited about telling us that's where we're going. I wish they could at least show a little sadness for the people they are so certain are going to end up there.

I have noticed, though, that they are consistent in their descriptions. They've all described hell as torment, fire that never stops burning, people wanting to die and not being able to. It sounds like a torture chamber. I don't see how God could do that to anyone. How can God claim to be such a pro at love and forgiveness and then turn around and send someone to hell? And if I understand correctly, once you're there, you never get out. There's an "in" door, but no "out" door.

As I told you the other night, I didn't grow up in a very loving home. I don't remember my parents ever saying, "I love you." That's probably why I have difficulty accepting love from others. I haven't been accustomed to being loved. I think my parents understood the word hate more than the word love. Sometimes the way they punished us was a nightmare. Nowadays we would call it child abuse, but back then people got away with it. At least my parents weren't relentless. They knew how to back off even though it often took them too long to do it.

From what I've heard of hell, it sounds like God never backs off. Once a person is in hell, God turns up the heat, and the person is there forever. I'm trying to find out how that fits in with his love, and I'm having a hard time putting it all together. I'll listen if you explain it to me, but please don't use the explanation I heard the other day. The person said, "God has a right to do anything he wants to do." That doesn't help my impression of God one bit!

I'm sure I'm not the only one with these feelings. The few conversations I've had with my friends tell me that. Don't you ever struggle with this problem?

Brian

Looking at Brian

To reach non-Christians does not mean believers must be good talkers; it means believers must be good listeners. As they listen, they should pay close attention not only to what non-Christians are saying but also to what they are not saying.

The fact that hell is so much on Brian's mind says something. Undoubtedly, he's struggling with feelings of guilt for wrong things he's done. Comments he's made would indicate that down deep he probably wants to feel loved by God. At the same time, he's wondering two things. First, how does he escape being punished for his wrongs? And second, how many right things must he do to make up for his wrongs? As he contemplates those two issues, we can understand how he wonders, "How could a loving God send someone to hell?"

Playing down the reality of hell is neither biblical nor loving! Hell is real, and Brian must understand its reality. At the same time, he needs to understand why it is real and that if he goes there it will not be because he is getting what he deserves but because he made a conscious choice.

Many people's impressions of God are based on their experiences with their human fathers. If their human father was a tyrant, they see God the same way. If their human father was loving and all-embracing, they again see God as the same. Since Brian didn't experience the love of a human father, he struggles with whether there is any love in God, especially a God who punishes sin. It is the presentation of the cross and the resurrection that will show God saying to Brian in the clearest way, "I love you, I love you, I love you."

Reaching non-Christians doesn't mean you have to share all your dirty laundry with them. But it does help when you feel free to relate areas of your past or present life of which you're not particularly proud. In so doing, you help them to realize that you're somebody who cares, and that if God could help you, He can help them. You'll notice Brian did not mention the abortion in his letter. It's often difficult for people to bring up a sin so grievous as abortion. Brian needs to understand that the God you are talking about has no limits to His love or forgiveness. Then, as the Holy Spirit works, he'll be able to understand that regardless of how dark some parts of his past have been (even the parts not shared), his future with Christ could not be any brighter.

Responding to Brian

Dear Brian,

I know you've struggled with some issues about God for some time. I appreciate you, Brian, and I want to help you understand. I'm glad you were interested and cared enough to say something about it. Although you are disturbed about something, at least you're willing to talk about it.

May I ask a favor of you? Toward the beginning of the New Testament there is a book called John. Take the next month and, beginning with the first chapter, read one chapter of that book each day. I'm recommending that book because of all the sixty-six books in the Bible, that is the one that will help you the most at this time. I'm asking you to read it because I want you to see the major thrust of Christ's ministry. While Christ was on earth, He was not scaring people out of going to hell with bad news; instead, he was inviting people to heaven with good news. He spoke more about hell than anyone else in the Bible, but that was not the major thrust of His ministry. He didn't earn His reputation as a "friend of sinners" by being harsh. He earned it by being loving and kind and extending to people like us love, hope, and forgiveness. If you read one chapter of the book of John each day, I think you will see what I mean. His message and ministry were not trying to scare people out of hell but inviting them to receive eternal life so they could live with Him in heaven.

If it bothers you how some people speak of hell, I wish you could understand how it grieves the Lord. People are right in saying there is a hell and even in describing what it is like, but they should do it with concern and compassion. Anything else fails to convey the love God has for those who might spend eternity there.

That's right: love. God does love them. That's why He went to the length He did. The very fact that He is holy and perfect demands that He must punish sin. A "slap on the wrist" is not enough. Due to its awful nature, sin is punishable by death. And death is more than an experience in which the heart stops and life on earth is over. Death is eternal separation from God.

Fortunately for us, God let His perfect Son, Jesus Christ, who never knew any sin—no wrong thoughts, bad words, un-kind attitudes, or evil actions—die on a cross, where you and I should have been punished. Christ actually took our place on a cross. The nails that should have been driven through our hands and feet were, instead, driven through His. You mentioned the punishments your parents used to give you, but even your parents wouldn't let you be punished for someone else's sin. Bear in mind, Christ didn't have to suffer for your sin—He loved you enough to do it. When God brought His Son up from the grave on the third day, He was providing the proof that, having punished sin, He could now extend forgive-ness and eternal life to anybody, anywhere. There is no sin that He cannot forgive and no person that He will not accept.

Let's suppose that you and I reject His offer. What we would be doing is saying to God, "I reject what Jesus Christ did in my place as my substitute." Therefore, He has no choice but to let us pay for our own sin, through eternal separation from Him in what the Bible calls hell.

Do you see my point, Brian? Those who go to hell are going there of their own choosing because they have rejected God and His free offer. He has not rejected them; instead, they have rejected Him.

May I give an analogy that will help? God blessed the two of you a year ago with a little boy. You love that little boy so much that you'd do anything for him. Forbid the thought, but suppose that when Douglas is twenty-one, he begins a wayward life and eventually murders someone. Your state sentences him to die in the electric chair. Suppose that you could walk into his cell the morning he is to be executed and offer to take his place. That's how great your love is for him. In so doing, you explain that he can be a free and forgiven man. Much to your surprise, he pushes you aside, walks to the electric chair, and receives the punishment for his horrible crime himself. Did you not love him enough? Would you accept the accusation, "If you really loved your son, you wouldn't have allowed that to happen"? Hardly! You did not reject him; he rejected you.

There is a hell, Brian, and it's even worse than you've ever heard it described. I couldn't live with my own conscience if I didn't tell you that, because that is what the Bible says. Those who spend eternity there will do so because they've rejected God's offer of forgiveness and eternal life. That's why, putting the responsibility where it belongs, the Bible says, "He came to His own, and His own did not receive Him. But as many as received Him, to them He gave the right to become children of God, even to those who believe in His name." You'll find those verses in that book of John.

You've had a lot of hard circumstances in your life. On top of that, I think that sometimes the mistakes of the past haunt you. You said to me the other day, "If you knew me better, you might not want to call me a friend." But you don't know some of the events in my past that I'm not proud of, either. When I was in my late teens I had a brush with the law that I've never told you about. Another fellow and I thought we'd try a little stealing. Little did we know that the cameras were on us. Because the owner of the store decided not to press charges, we got off easy. But I don't mind telling you I was scared. I don't know yet what possessed me to do such a thing. When I came to Christ, He helped me to put all that behind me. For the last five years I've been living in forgiveness. If He forgave me, He will forgive you, too. One of the most exciting things about the Christian life is not simply knowing I have been forgiven and am going to heaven, although that in itself is enough. But since I've come to Christ, I know He's with me all day every day. Disappointments don't seem nearly as big, and bad days don't seem nearly as bad with Him there.

I have a few more thoughts I'd like to share, but I have to hit the sack. Our company is installing some new systems and everybody has been exhausted trying to figure them out. I'm beat! I'll write you again and share some more thoughts that might be helpful. Whatever we do, let's keep talking.

Blake

Kristie's Struggle

Church might excite God, but it doesn't
excite me. I just don't fit in.

Who Is Kristie?

Kristie is a homemaker in western Oregon. Raised in a rural community, she and her husband, Bud, both enjoy a small-town atmosphere. Having high standards and having come from a church background, she thinks of herself as "religious." Attending church, in her mind, is a must, even though she's not thought through the why but only the where. She doesn't think analytically, and she tends to lump everything together without making important distinctions.

Listening to Kristie

Dear Kathy,

I'm a reverent, God-fearing woman. I'm certainly not in the camp of those who reduce God to a curse word. My mind is boggled by those who wonder if God truly exists. If I were God, I wouldn't be nearly as patient with people as he is. Those who deny his existence would probably hold a rock in their hand and deny it's a rock. Everywhere I go and everywhere I look, I see "billboards" that say God is real. The outdoors of Oregon has his fingerprints all over it. In my opinion, the truth that God exists is a no-brainer.

However, I would like to discuss something I find discouraging and disturbing. You've always been someone I can talk to, so let me share my thoughts. This town in Oregon has become home to us ever since Bud was promoted and transferred here two years ago by his computer company. It is just the right size and everything seems perfect. We love it! It's something how much it rains up here, but we don't mind. The kids can play in our yard, and I don't have to worry about their safety. And we have just the right size shopping mall, although some wouldn't call it that. It is an ideal "little America." Bud was adamant that this was his last company transfer, and he even dared to tell his boss that.

But finding a church has been a different story. Bud and I attend about half of the time. We do miss a lot, but Sunday is our only day to do things together as a family. Since we go a lot more than some people do, we don't feel too bad about it. We have yet to find a church, though, where we feel comfortable. It's not that there aren't enough to choose from. We are surprised how many churches there are in this size community, but I wouldn't call what we've seen much of a choice. I think circus would be a better name for where we've been than church. It doesn't matter where we attend, we have to laugh to keep from crying.

We probably aren't sure what we need in a church or even what we're looking for, but just look at the places we've visited. What a fiasco they've been.

The first one took the cake. In one message, the minister pointed out everything that was wrong with society. I think he would have made a better politician than a preacher. I'll never know how his voice didn't give out. He shouted most of his message. Since our opinions in certain areas were certainly not the same as his, we knew within two Sundays that that was not the place for us.

The next church didn't like our kids. They never came out and said that, but they made it pretty obvious. Our son's hair was too long, and our daughter's skirt was too short. We realized we had been ostracized. Getting ready for church meant having a family argument, as well as a "dress rehearsal," and we knew we'd better exit fast. We'd never seen a church with more rules and regulations. The Ten Commandments at times seem a little stiff, but that church added about forty more to the ten.

The next one we tried was like a mortuary. Don't ask me why we even went back there. In the four times we went, we never met a single soul. It was like the inside of a funeral parlor. Every time we walked out, we felt that we were leaving a scene from The Night of the Living Dead.

Church people can be the best prize fighters around. The next church proved that. We were shocked when the man in the seat ahead of us whispered to his wife, "I wish the pastor would resign. Then we could get somebody good for a change." Her response was no better. She pointed to the couple ahead of them and said, "Now, if they left, that would be better yet!" I could tell that the couple heard her. And we could sense that several people were angry during the whole service. I have no idea why. Once more, it felt better walking out than walking in. I've recently heard that that church had a major split. I'm not sure what was involved in their "split," but it didn't help God's reputation in this community.

Let's just skip the next one we tried, because we felt all they wanted us to do was to turn our bank account over to them. I've never held my purse any tighter than in that church. Bud did the same thing with his wallet and credit cards. So, here we are at the church we're attending now. It's probably the least of all evils, but it's still nothing to write home about. There's no youth program, the music is boring, and the one-hour church service seems like two.

I'm sure I've lost all chance to be God's church promotion chairwoman. Church has done nothing but leave us empty. I know going to church is an essential part of getting to heaven, but what does God expect us to do? Which place does he want us to put up with?

Kristie

Looking at Kristie

Kristie has to be faced head-on with the difference between being a Christian and being a churchgoer. Otherwise, she'll never see the distinction. However, since she is religious, it is important to "come up from under her" not "down from on top of her." She is the type who would be easily threatened by the gospel.

Saying to Kristie that "the issue is Christ, not church" is not enough. One must explain what that means, making the gospel abundantly clear—Christ died for us and rose so that, through simple faith in Him, we can enjoy the free gift of life eternal. Using an illustration from a life experience with which a non-Christian is acquainted is often a big help.

With anyone, but particularly with religious people, use your own testimony whenever possible. That assures them that you are not trying to be accusatory; you are simply trying to help.

Kristie is up front in expressing her concerns. Such people usually appreciate that in others. It's important that they sense you are direct because you care, not simply that you care to be direct.

Responding to Kristie

Dear Kristie,

We were excited to hear how much you're enjoying life in Oregon. Richard and I laughed when you talked about just the right size shopping mall. You and I are so much alike. As soon as you described things there, I wanted Richard to quit his job so we could pack our bags and move there! But he says he's into sun, not rain. Oh well!

I'm sorry you're having a hard time finding a church. I certainly give you an A for your effort to find one. As you mentioned, you aren't in church every Sunday, but you have attended a lot of churches. There's an element in all of that which bothers me for you. I fear there's something you don't understand.

There are things you and Bud are getting wrong. I could tell by your comment, "I know going to church is an essential part of getting to heaven." My concern is how well you understand what the Bible teaches. At this point in your lives, God is not saying, "Come to church." Instead, what He's saying is, "Come to Christ."

In our last phone conversation, you said, "We are not half as bad as a lot of people we know." God doesn't compare you with anyone you know. He compares you with His Son, Jesus Christ, who was absolutely perfect. Compared with Him, you and I are what He declares us to be—sinners. The punishment He must render for sin is everlasting separation from Him.

That is what the cross was all about. God's perfect Son took your punishment. Bud told me about the crossing guard who stepped out in front of a speeding motorist to push a child to safety two miles from your house. In so doing, he died. Your whole town has apparently been talking about it. Bud told me your comment to him was: "If he hadn't died, that child would have." That's the very thing I want you and Bud to understand. The punishment for sin is death and eternal separation from God. Had God's Son, Jesus, not died in your place, He would have to punish you. But through Christ's death and resurrection, He can now forgive you instead of punishing you.

You, Bud, your family, and everybody else must trust one Person to save you—the Person who died for you. Eternal life cannot be earned. It can only be received as a free gift through His Son. The Bible declares, "He who believes in the Son has everlasting life." You will find that verse in the third chapter of the book of John.

Trusting Christ to save you at this point is of the greatest importance. Church cannot save you. Only Christ can. Most people don't understand that, and I'm concerned that perhaps you don't, either. Richard and I were married for several years

and went to church all that time before we came to understand the difference between going to church and becoming
a Christian. It was a friend of Richard's from work who cared
enough to explain it to us. At first, we balked at what he was
saying, but when he showed us that what he was saying was
exactly what the Bible says, we couldn't argue.

As for churches, don't expect to find a perfect one. Sometimes, even for Christians, church isn't nearly as exciting as it
could be or as they'd like it to be. What you have found, for
the most part, is dishonoring to God. His place of worship
is not meant to be a place for fighting, nor does He expect it
to be a place for pleading for money. Don't misunderstand
me. God is not embarrassed by money, and many of the stories Jesus Christ told concerned the use of money. What a
Christian does with his money is often an indication of how
much he has grown as a Christian. Church, however, is to
be a place where His Word is studied and where His people
pray and worship together.

I have an idea. When you get a chance, get out your
Bible and turn to the New Testament portion. Find Acts
2:42. Concerning the early church, the Bible says, "And they
continued steadfastly in the apostles' doctrine and fellowship,
in the breaking of bread, and in prayers." That's what His
church is to be about. So look for a church that teaches the
Bible, where people pray and have fellowship together, and
where they remember Christ's death through communion. If
it has all that, you can help it with what it doesn't have—like
a good youth program. Don't attend God's places of worship
simply wondering, "What can they do for me?" He wants you
to serve and not look for others to serve you. If the church is
not all that you'd like it to be, God can help you strengthen
weak areas. Just be patient and keep looking. We found our
present church when our son was invited to a youth program
by one of his friends from school.

Kristie, put things in their proper order. Richard's friend
who led us to Christ really got through to us when he said,
"Religion will take you to church, but only God's Son can

take you to heaven." Please share this letter with Bud. I hope both of you understand I'm trying to help. I don't mean to hurt your feelings.

Kathy

Kevin's Struggle

*A lot has happened since I first came
to God, but something is still missing.
Please help me understand what it is.*

Who Is Kevin?

Kevin moved to New England to take a job with a major corporation. Soon, his life was going down the tubes at breakneck speed. His marriage was headed for the rocks, and alcohol consumed his life. Like many other people, he had an experience with God that changed his life. Also, like many people, he still has not come to grips with the meaning of the gospel.

Listening to Kevin

Dear Chip,

Wow! Was I ever headed down the wrong track. A lot of people must have known. It all started three years ago when we got word that my nephew, who was eighteen at the time, had been diagnosed with an extremely rare and fatal heart disease. It was the most devastating blow we had ever had. Since my wife and I haven't been able to have any children of our own, Robert was special to us. You know my brother and me, and you also know we've always been close, so naturally we were close to Robert as well. In many ways, we were closer to him than most parents are to their own children. We went to all of his football games, showered him with presents, and never missed an opportunity to be with him. I remember my brother laughingly saying, "Sometimes I get confused if he's your son or mine."

Since in many ways he was our only child, too, we just couldn't handle his passing. I wasn't upset with God—just with life. Why does it have to be so unfair? Robert had a football scholarship, a mind that wouldn't quit, and, to top it all off, he had looks and manners, too! He knew where he was going with his life. Losing Robert was devastating. Although alcohol had never been one of my weaknesses, like it was my brother's, at that time I used it to numb my feelings more nights than I care to remember.

Shortly after that, everything disintegrated at work. The corporation I worked for announced major changes, and I was on the "out" list. Financially, we could manage things for awhile, but I didn't have the energy to look for a job. Robert was all I could think about. Stacy was handling things better than I was, but even she started to fall apart. We'd never had a strong marriage, and, before I knew it, divorce papers were being filed.

That's when it hit me—three strikes and you're out. I woke up one morning with a hangover and saw the rest of my life before me. I have a feeling God helped me to see it. I knew that if I didn't get things turned around, my life was over. Only God knows how much I had been contemplating suicide. Don't ask me why, because to this day I do not know, but I dropped out of bed, got down on my knees, and yelled, "Oh, God, help me." I've never cried so hard in my life. I guess I just knew I couldn't go on any longer without his help.

Some people say talking to God is like talking to a brick wall, but he sure came through for me. I got out my wife's Bible, and I decided I was going to let God turn my life around. I still can't believe what he did. There was even a change in Stacy that could only have come from God. I never thought she would give our marriage another chance, but she stopped the divorce proceedings and started talking about working out our problems and staying together. We've had a better marriage in the last two months than we've had in the last twenty years.

Then—what a shocker! An old high school friend called to offer me a job with his company. I have never loved a job more than this one. It's perfect for me. I'm reading the Bible, we are going to church, and I haven't had a drink for three months. There isn't a single day that goes by that I don't think about Robert, but somehow I think I can go on.

But in spite of all that, something is still missing. I still feel sad and lonely on the inside. Do I just need more time to work beyond the grief of Robert's death? I'm confused about how my brother and his wife have handled their own son's passing so well. They cry at times when they talk about him, but they didn't fall apart the way I did. Do you have any ideas about what I need to do? I could talk to my brother. I think he could help. As close as we are, somehow spiritual things have always been hard for us to discuss. I was pretty negative with him years ago when he told me he became a Christian. I think he is afraid to approach the subject now. I'd rather talk to you if I can.

Kevin

Looking at Kevin

Evangelism has many exciting moments. One of the most exciting is when we meet a non-Christian who is so open he's like fruit ready to fall off a limb.

Those people, though, are sometimes easy to talk to and sometimes difficult. They can be easy because of their openness. They can be difficult because emotions or excitement makes them talk instead of listen. Saving faith is based on understanding the gospel message and then simply trusting Christ alone to save us. Unless a person understands what he is doing, he cannot make a genuine decision about Christ.

Relatives are sometimes the hardest to reach because we fear rejection. For years, one thing I've counseled believers to do is to ask God to send someone in addition to themselves to talk to them. Someone outside the family, in a warm and receptive environment, can sometimes do more than someone in the family. Bear in mind that we could be the "someone" for whom a relative in another family has been praying for many years. A new face, a new voice, and different words can do a lot to help.

One mistake believers often make in a situation like the one before us is to assume that Kevin has come to Christ and simply has other problems he needs to deal with. These problems could be anything from grief or midlife crisis to not enough companionship. Many times such a person has come toward God, but they haven't come to God.

Complimenting everything that has happened and sharing the excitement are most important. Then Kevin must be shown, not what he has discovered, but what he has still missed. With Kevin's openness and the Lord working in his heart and mind, we have the tremendous opportunity of leading him to the Savior. His testimony will then be, "Something was missing, and God used you to show me what it was."

Responding to Kevin

Dear Kevin,

You're right. Something is missing. I have no doubt I can help you see what it is. This could be the most exciting day of your life. It's a day some of your friends have been praying for, including your own brother. As you can imagine, sometimes relatives have the most difficulty talking to members of their own family, even though they care so much for them.

I'm glad you don't blame God for Robert's death. That is what a lot of people do. They don't understand that although nothing can happen apart from God allowing it, there is never any evil intent in what He does or allows. If we could see life from His vantage point, things would make sense to you and me that don't make any sense now.

As you mentioned, I'm fortunate to know you and your brother well. When I was talking with him the other day, he told me something exciting. Think back to a time six years ago, just before Robert turned fifteen. You and Stacy noticed a dramatic change in their family, but you never knew what did it. In three words, "God did it."

Your brother tells me that your family recognized you as the morally straight one in your family. Your brother had always been the "wild card." For years, he drank heavily, spent little time with Robert, and was irresponsible in just about everything. Knowing him now, it's hard for me even to imagine what he was like. Then God brought a business acquaintance into your brother's life. That man told him about something I'm going to explain to you. Your brother and his entire family came to Christ. Robert is with the Lord now, and one day your brother and his wife will be, too. That's why they have handled Robert's death so well. They haven't "lost" Robert. They know where he is. I want you to understand what I'm about to tell you, so you and Stacy will one day be with Robert and, more importantly, with Christ, forever. That's right, Kevin—forever.

You acknowledge that God is the reason for the change in your life, and I'm glad you've started studying the Bible. There is not a situation or problem you will face in life for which the Bible does not give all the wisdom and guidance needed. Reading the Bible is the main way God talks to us.

Take your Bible and open it to John 19:30. When God's Son died on a cross, what did He say? "It is finished!" What He meant by that is, "I have done everything that needed to be done to secure your forgiveness and for you to have eternal life. I have made the complete payment for your sins."

It appears that everything spiraled downhill for you after Robert's death. You mentioned one time that your grief was so overwhelming that you even became irresponsible in paying your bills. Your utility company threatened to cut off your electricity, and in the dead of winter with fifteen inches of snow on the ground, that would have been bad news. That must have been around the time God started to get your attention, because you began to notice your own irresponsible behavior. It might have fit your brother years ago, but it wasn't like you. I forget the amount, but I think you told me that you took three hundred dollars to the electric company and gave it to them. They accepted your money and marked your bill "paid in full."

Two thousand years ago, Jesus Christ died on a hill called Calvary. On a cross, He took our debt of sins and, before a holy God, died in our place. The moment He did, our debt before God was "paid in full." Jesus arose on the third day, a resurrection that proved He had conquered sin and the grave. We have to receive what God has done by trusting His Son to save us.

You have come near God, Kevin, but you still haven't come to Him. I think that you want Him to accept you because of your daily Bible reading, prayers, and the way you have reformed your life. He is aware of those changes, but He cannot accept you on that basis. He can only accept you based on what His Son did on the cross for you. He did not die to help you get to heaven. He died as your substitute, and He is your only way to heaven. If you reject His Son by depending on a life of good deeds to get you there, you are in no better condition than the murderer who rejects God's Son through a life of crime for which he never asks forgiveness.

When you trust Christ as your Savior—notice that I use the word Savior, your only way to heaven—He'll immediately give you the free gift of life eternal, and you will be a part of His forever family. That's what's missing, Kevin. You know all about God, but you still don't know God. Today that can change. In the privacy of your own heart, just tell God that you know you are a sinner who cannot save yourself, and that right now you are putting your trust in Christ alone to save you. The moment you trust Christ, Kevin, you are His. Don't make it difficult when it's so simple.

Your brother told me about that first conversation with

him when you became pretty upset. He wanted you to un-derstand how he and his family became Christians. I know he's been praying for you and Stacy even though he hasn't mentioned the subject again. You're right. Spiritual things are sometimes harder for family members to discuss. Once you come to Christ, you can help Stacy understand. She respects you even more now because of the change she's seen in you. I think she'd be very receptive to hearing all about what I've explained to you.

I can't wait to hear from you. Regardless of how many people come to Christ every day, each one is always special. This includes you, too, Kevin. Call me and let me know when you've settled it. I'll be as excited as you. Once you've trusted Christ, we could meet together and I could help you start growing as a Christian. Could I do that for you? I would really like to if you'd let me.

Chip

Bruce's Struggle

Why would a happy person need Jesus?

Who Is Bruce?

Bruce is from an upper-class New York City neighborhood with an all-American family. Nothing stands in the way of his being an executive for his company within five years. A high achiever with a tremendous amount of pride and self-sufficiency, Bruce lives and breathes the philosophy, "Eat, drink, and be merry."

Listening to Bruce

Dear Dusty,

I enjoyed our talk the other day, but I'm sure I frustrated you. I'm not trying to be difficult or smart, but let's face it, I just don't need God.

I don't know how things could go any better for me. I've just gotten my second promotion in eighteen months. My boss told me that I'm the first one who has risen up the corporate ladder that fast, and I'm not surprised. After all, I deserve it. I've worked hard for the company. I've lived by the policy, "Do unto others as you would have them do unto you," and it's paid off for me. I stroke others' backs, and they stroke mine. At this rate, I'm going to be looking at a six-figure income within five years. That's when I'll start giving orders instead of taking them.

My job is not the only thing going great for me. I have an attractive wife and a good marriage. Sure, we have our arguments, but what couple doesn't? We were saying the other night that our marriage is better than most couples we know. I take her out to a really nice restaurant once a month. Wait until my income increases, then I'm really going to splurge and let her experience the best!

Look at my kids. Sherry just finished eighth grade and has it all together—looks, brains, everything. She's definitely a chip off the old block. You can't blame me for being a bit proud. When we turn her loose to date, the guys are going to be lining up at the door. My son, Tim, is no slouch, either. His coach is already talking to him about a football scholarship. He has the brains to get any job he wants. Both of them have told me I've given them everything they could want. Sure, Tim seems a little depressed lately. But he'll be alright. That's just the price of adolescence. His determination will carry him through anything. I know I haven't spent anywhere close to the time with him I should, but I've taught him well: "Whatever you want, go for it. Don't let anything or anyone stop you." It seems as though life just goes my way. You've got to hand it to me, Dusty. I'm an optimistic guy. I expect things to go right. Positive thinking has done me a lot of good.

Don't put me into the category of those who feel God doesn't exist. I'm sure he does, and I don't doubt he's helped a lot of people. But he's really more for the down-and-outer and the fellow whose life is a mess. I think it's great the way he helps people like that. I just don't need him myself. To put it as simply as I can, I'm happy with everything—my life, my job, my income, my family, my church life, everything.

Speaking of church, I know I'm only there once or twice a month, but, in my opinion, too much of anything, particularly religion, isn't good for you. Take Carl, for example. He really went all out for this religion stuff. Everybody said what a happy and changed guy he was. Some people even said he had something they thought I needed. They aren't saying that anymore. Carl committed suicide two weeks ago. It really shook a lot of people up. I pity Carl's family, and we'll try to do something to help. I don't like to be around a family where someone has died. That always makes me feel a bit eerie. But maybe we could loan them the keys to our place by the Jersey shore and let them have a weekend getaway.

I'm glad I've thrown that midlife crisis stuff out the window. I'm not having a midlife crisis. I'm having a midlife celebration. So thanks for offering your services or spiritual advice, as I guess you'd call it, but frankly, there are other people you should give your attention to who really need God. My philosophy of life is simple: when things are going great, don't rattle the cage.

Please don't think I'm criticizing you or anything you've said. I just don't want you to waste your time. Religion is simply not something I need.

Bruce

Looking at Bruce

It will probably do absolutely no good to try to convince Bruce that he's not happy. Even though a believer would realize that Bruce does not have happiness the way Christ describes it, convincing Bruce of that is next to impossible!

Instead, we need to put the emphasis where the Bible puts it—on eternal life. Paul the apostle even said, "If in this life only we have hope in Christ, we are of all men the most pitiable" (1 Cor. 15:19).

There isn't a person alive who, in quieter moments of reflection, doesn't ponder the fact that he has no certainty of life after death. Famous and wealthy people have testified in publications such as Time magazine that the one thing that bothers them is the thought of death and what might happen

Responding to Bruce

Dear Bruce,

You're right. You certainly don't lack self-confidence, and I wouldn't accuse you of being someone who lives as if God doesn't exist. In the short time I've known you, you've always believed in the existence of a Superior Being. Please don't think I'm trying to convince you that you're not really happy, that you only think you are. I'm not interested in doing that. Your definition of happiness says you have all you need—and more.

However, Bruce, I think you're terribly deceived, and I'll explain what I mean by that.

You pride yourself in your abilities and accomplishments—and you've done a lot. You've accomplished everything that matters when you look at life from a forty- to eighty-year span. But then what, Bruce? You mentioned the other night when we talked that, although you feel you have a "good shot" at going to heaven, you don't have the certainty of where you're going when you die. God's greatest concern is not the here and now. God's greatest concern is eternity. I've been wanting to talk to you before now. I feel as though every time I've tried to get close to you, you back away.

I'm glad you have all you have, but I do wish that you'd give God the credit for what you enjoy. Your children aren't merely the result of the relationship between Sarah and you. They came from God. He created them. Have you ever thought about that? What about the health you've enjoyed? Where do you think that came from? Now, what's going to happen when, all of a sudden, you come to the end of your life and it's your time to do what everyone does—die? Like everybody else, you have an appointment with God. And that's when your pride will not only be hurt, it will be crushed.

Why? Because you don't understand what God's Son, Jesus Christ, has done for you. You believe there is a hereafter—a very real heaven and hell. I've heard you say they exist. Because you've never looked at the Bible, though, you're convinced that after that. That is why Bruce must come to grips with the gospel message of the cross and the empty tomb. No other message offers and guarantees eternal life.

When speaking to non-Christians, what they don't say is even more important at times than what they do say. Bruce's comment about being uneasy around a family where death has occurred discloses his troubled feelings about the hereafter far more than he is willing to admit.

When we witness to a proud person such as Bruce, we must constantly pull into the conversation our own background and shortcomings. This helps to tear down the non-Christian's defenses, particularly someone with Bruce's arrogance. It helps him or her to be more receptive to our message. The theme of "Here's how God got through to me" reveals something about our own former hardness and helps others to look at themselves realistically. What they hear from us, then, is a testimony instead of a sermon.

When we are witnessing to non-Christians, every word and every facial expression becomes important. The reference Bruce made to the little time he has spent with his son is most revealing. The expression on his face tells how troubling that is to him. Watching facial expressions gives us an opportunity to speak to the person's hurts, especially in those moments when they are most transparent.

Carl's suicide needs to be clearly addressed, because it is so confusing and contradictory to the non-Christian. If Christ is the answer, why did Carl end his life instead of living it to the fullest? It appears to hurt the credibility of the Christian message and portrays the Christian life as nothing more than an emotional high that is "here today, gone tomorrow." We don't need to apologize for the situation, though. Just pointing out the reality of what may have happened shows that Christians can have a genuine, born-again experience and at the same time remain human enough to make some very regrettable decisions.

you can climb the ladder to heaven the way you've climbed the ladder at work—by your own effort. No way! You have done many good things in forty-three years, but you have done much that's wrong as well. Because God is a holy God, He has to punish sin. That means you are facing a separation from God that will last forever. I think that if I have any concern for you, I need to warn you. You are going to wish you had God in your life instead of having wealth, happiness, and a good family without Him. Look what His Son did for you. You deserve to be punished for your sins, but He took your place. He died as your substitute, not because you love Him, but because He loves you.

You give yourself credit for being a great dad, and although you've done a lot for your kids, you've also left a lot undone. At some moments you're more transparent than others. Do you remember what you told me at lunch about a year ago? You're right. Your daughter, Sherry, is very attractive. If I remember, you explained that she started to get "too close" to a young man who was walking her home from school. Knowing how your supervisor's daughter fell into an immoral situation and got pregnant outside of marriage, you transferred all those fears to Sherry. Remember how angry you told me you were? You told her if that ever happened to her, she'd be your daughter in name only. To this day you've been too proud to apologize to Sherry. Your concern was probably partially legitimate, but it was also exaggerated.

What's my point? God loves you, Bruce—regardless. He doesn't love people the way you and I do—based on what they've done. He loves them in spite of what they've done.

You seemed confused the other night when I told you that eternal life was a gift. You heard me right. Eternal life is free. But you have to trust Jesus Christ to save you—not your good behavior, good works, and many accomplishments. I like to pride myself on some of the things I've done, too. However, God cannot accept me because of those things. As sinners, we have to come to God, recognize that His Son died for us, taking the punishment for our sins. Three days later, He rose from the grave. For that reason, we must place our trust in Jesus Christ alone to save us and give us eternal life. If you did it right now, you would receive that free gift this very moment.

You mentioned Carl's passing and how "eerie" you feel around a family where death has occurred. You should feel eerie. Death is very serious, Bruce. If you recall, one of the reasons you had an opportunity for promotion was that your first supervisor, George, was killed in a car crash just two days before his fortieth birthday. What if that had been you? I have to warn you, you must come to God and trust His Son to save you. Otherwise, He must punish you for your sins through everlasting separation from Him.

By the way, could I caution you about something? You're sometimes quick to jump to conclusions. Carl didn't die from an overdose of religion. You're forgetting that I knew Carl, too. Carl came to Christ and trusted Christ as his Savior because a friend at work cared enough to talk to him about the Lord. Carl shared his testimony with me about two weeks before he died. What you and many others don't know is that Carl's daughter is in serious trouble with the law. I might as well tell you about it because it's about to hit the news. She got involved with the wrong people and started dealing drugs. They've postponed the hearing because of Carl's death, but she's facing some pretty serious charges. When Carl found out, it was more than he could handle. He blamed himself for it. He kept saying, "If I had only come to Christ sooner." God tells His children to bring all their problems to Him and He'll help them, but Carl, being a new Christian, didn't do that. He shouldered everything himself. In a moment of irrational thinking, he did something very foolish.

But do you know where the Bible says Carl is? He's in heaven! There is no question that he now knows committing suicide was the wrong thing to do, but he had come to Christ, and God doesn't reject anyone He's received. When a person is His, he's His forever. It has cost Carl in terms of the reward God could have otherwise given him, but since he trusted God's Son as his Savior, he's better off now than you will be if you don't come to Christ. Please consider what I'm telling you. I say what I do because I care about you.

When Carl died, I was at his funeral, too. The pastor said something that I know made a lot of people think, unless they simply dismissed it from their minds. He's a good pastor who teaches what the Bible says. Looking at all of Carl's family and friends, he said, "Carl's life ended abruptly, but we know where he is. If your life ended abruptly would we know where you were?" It was that kind of question that, years ago, brought me to Christ when I was almost killed in that work accident I told you about. God had to use something pretty severe to get my attention.

Again, Bruce, I don't deny you're happy, and I'm happy for you. What concerns me, though, is that all your happiness is wrapped primarily around things—the job, the car, the money, the house. But what will any of that mean two seconds after you die? If you come to Christ, He'll show you what real happiness is—the kind of happiness your father-in-law has. You know what everyone says about him. They say, "He must be the happiest person I know." Of course, materially and financially, you have ten times what he'll ever have. The difference is that he has a relationship with Christ. His happiness has a lot more contentment tied in with it than yours does. He knows who is important and not simply what.

You referred to Tim's depression. It may be more serious than you think. You're right when you say you've given your children everything they've ever wanted, but there are some things money can't buy. There might be times when Tim gets depressed because you don't spend time with him like his buddy's dad does with his son. I know it bothers you too, otherwise, you wouldn't mention it so often. You've been promising Tim for six months that you'd take him fishing, but you keep putting it off. I'll bet you Tim couldn't care less if you go fishing or not; he just wants to be with you. I know I'm preaching at you, Bruce, but it's only because I'm trying to help. I don't want you to make the mistakes I did. I never spent the time with my boy that I should have, and I still regret it. Now that all of us have straightened things out with the Lord, he's forgiven me, and am I ever grateful for that! My brother-in-law, whose son is retarded, understood love more than I did. He always loved his son for who he was, not for what he might become. That's another person God used to get my attention. Give Tim the time he needs. Remember, the questions that interest God are a lot different from those that interest people. Some of your friends are quick to say, "How's your job?" God likes to start by saying, "How's your family?"

My frustration probably shows more than I'd like it to. If you were a "down-and-outer," you'd be more apt to understand why you need Christ.

Please don't let your happiness deceive you. You have done a lot and you have a lot. But of what possible importance could all of that be if you don't know that you're going to be with God forever when your life ends? I really care about you, Bruce, and I care about what happens to you.

Dusty

letter twelve

Diana's Struggle

If God is so great,
why are his people so awful?

Who Is Diana?

Diana is a homemaker who lives in a small town in the Midwest. Approaching her late forties, she is beginning to slow down and think about some of the deeper issues of life. Most people would call her a God-fearing person with a tremendous respect for what is honest and decent. Her husband works for the local telephone company. They have two children: a married daughter and a son still at home. Like many people, they go to church on occasions such as Christmas and Easter. Her confusion about Christians has caused her to be a bit confused about God.

Listening to Diana

Dear Marsha,

When you talk about God, do you ever get embarrassed? Most people I know who claim to know God say, as you do, that he is great. They seem to be trying to give me the impression that to miss out on knowing him is to miss out on life. The two words they use most are the same two you use—power and love. Another one of my friends who is also a Christian told me a few weeks ago at work that if I would just come to God, all my problems would be over. You and she are two of the best salespeople God has.

Can I ask you a question? If God is as great as everyone says he is, why are some of his people so awful? They are often downright hypocritical. Now, I admit that you are different, and that's why when you talk I listen. But you're the exception. Another Christian friend of mine irritates me so often. I don't trust her at all. I can't prove it, but I think that she is getting involved with a married man.

Since God supposedly sees everything, he must have seen the article in Time magazine years ago about Mike Tyson. As you know, Brad is a boxing fan and has followed Tyson's career, so he kept the article. It's dated February 24, 1992. I know Tyson was a good boxer, but I laughed when I read that "he was the most dangerous man in sports, the once and [we supposed] future heavyweight champion of the world, whose conquests included forty professional boxers and countless women." Then the story told of an Indianapolis jury finding Tyson guilty of rape and two counts of criminal sexually deviant conduct, stemming from a beauty pageant he attended. He apparently raped one of the contestants. A line in the article explains what I'm getting at. Time said, "When Desiree Washington met Mike Tyson at a beauty pageant last July, she saw not the thug of tabloid length, but a young man wearing a Together with Christ button who was praying with Jesse Jackson. Tyson, it appears, saw a late-night snack."

I understand that Tyson now ridicules the Bible and Christianity, but that sure isn't what he was doing at the time. Marsha, you know I could add many more examples of hypocrisy to that one. Saying one thing and doing another has been rampant in Christianity. In fact, I've read the results of a survey taken among those who don't know God and don't care to. They were asked if they felt Christians were any different from them. Their answer was a big fat no, except for two things: one, Christians go to church more often; and two, Christians are more negative! Do you know what an attorney friend told Brad and me the other day? He said, "When I do business with a non-Christian, I take another attorney with me. When I do business with a Christian, I take two!"

As far as I am concerned, Christians are some of the most selfish, uncaring, hypocritical, and immoral people in existence. If I see a reference to God on a bumper sticker, I try to stay as far away from the car and the driver as I can. And if someone told me that the woman with the driver was not his wife but someone he's having an affair with, I wouldn't be the least bit surprised.

I've probably rubbed enough salt into the wound, but look at some of God's most famous spokesmen from the recent past, those televangelists for example. Wow! Did they ever preach about God! Of course, the whole time, a couple of them were hoping nobody would find out what everybody eventually did. Apparently, if they weren't around the one they loved, they just loved the one they were around. Their burden for the world was really a burden for the women of the world. Pardon the sarcasm!

I think perhaps God ought to have a clean-up campaign and eliminate those who are hypocrites. I'm convinced, though, that if he did, many of his people would no longer exist.

Diana

Looking at Diana

Diana, like most non-Christians, is a normal human being who does two things that cloud her judgment.

One is that she quickly jumps to conclusions. She judges a book by its cover. She has looked so much at the lifestyles of Christians that she has never heard their message. In no way does that justify their lifestyles, but can't an ambassador of good news have a wrong life although he carries the right message? Can't a president of the United States sign good legislation even though his life leaves a lot to be desired? If a cultist has the kind of commendable life that could put some Christians to shame, do we accept his message as being true? If a non-Christian does not make a distinction between a person's lifestyle and his message, confusion will always reign. Diana must learn to make this distinction.

That's why she must be confronted with the crucifixion and the resurrection of Christ. Nothing she sees in the lives of Christians changes the fact that Christ died for her and rose again. The issue is first and foremost not what Christians have done, but what He, the Savior, did for her on a cross. At the same time, Diana must be given credit for what she sees and for making the observations she has made. To deny that some Christians are hypocritical or to become defensive about it would do no good.

Diana's second mistake is that she is prejudicial, as most people are. Even though she credits Marsha as being different, she talks more about those who do not live the way she thinks Christians should live. That is a common error non-Christians make—seeing and talking about the ones they want to see and talk about. I've discovered that they may know five Christians who live proper lives. But if they have met or know one who doesn't, they capitalize on the one, not on the five. I've asked them, "Do you know any Christians whom you do respect for the way they live?" With a look of chagrin on their faces, most of the time they have admitted that they do. But they focus on the hypocritical ones and not on the ones trying to live Christlike lives.

Non-Christians are often inconsistent in their thinking, as all of us can be at times. Diana respects her attorney friend as being trustworthy even though many attorneys are not noted as being such. Yet she does not consider Christians trustworthy even though she knows one who is!

Responding to Diana

Dear Diana,

You're exactly right. Some of the people who claim to know God are selfish, uncaring, hypocritical, and immoral. I'm not proud of that, and I'm sure God isn't either. I'm not going to make excuses for what they do. It's just plain sin. But there are a few things you're overlooking, Diana, and I'll guarantee that God's biggest enemy, Satan, will do his best to keep you from seeing what I'm about to tell you.

You keep referring to people who know God. Please try to understand that there is an enormous difference between people who say they know God and people who actually do. One thing is stressed in the Bible over and over: eternal life is a free gift. A person doesn't get to heaven by going to church, living well, being baptized, keeping the commandments, or taking the sacraments. Instead, he must come to God as a sinner and recognize that God's Son, Jesus Christ, paid for his wrongs on the cross and rose on the third day. Then he must simply put his trust in Christ alone to save him. The moment he does, God gives that person the free gift His Son's death on the cross has already paid for—eternal life. But God does more than that. Just as the Bible promises, God then comes into his life and gives him the ability to live a different kind of life, a life where he has the power to resist temptation and do what's right instead of what's wrong.

Like you, many people miss that simple message. The only difference is that they go to church on Sunday. Since they don't actually know Christ, because they have not trusted Him to save them, their lives are no different from anybody else's. The power or ability to live a different kind of life is not available to them because He is not actually their Savior. In fact, they sometimes use religion to cover up their sin. Please make a distinction in your mind between people who actually know Him and those who only say they do. Many people who say they know God will be separated from Him forever, because the truth is, they don't know Him. Instead of trusting Christ and His death on the cross as their only way to heaven, they are instead relying on their good works, religious efforts, or kind deeds to save them.

I need to explain something else, and I can use your own family as an example. When a person trusts God's Son, Jesus Christ, as Savior, he or she is forever His child. God won't take back what He wrote in the book of John in the Bible: "As many as received Him, to them He gave the right to become children of God, to those who believe in His name." But children can lose their closeness to a father, and some of God's children lose their closeness to Him. When that happens, they do things they know are wrong and, unfortunately, at times they don't care. That doesn't change the fact that they are still His children, but He is not proud of their behavior. Since you are a mother, you can understand that.

Do you remember when your daughter, Carol, turned thirteen? Suddenly, she seemed to change. You and she experienced four very difficult years. I don't have to remind you what she did or how the neighbors talked. Your first concern was for her, but you were also concerned for your and Brad's reputation in the community. I tried to encourage you during that time, but I'm not sure I helped much. Although you weren't too proud of her, you never disowned her. In fact, sometimes you had to discipline her rather severely.

In the same way, God loves His children, and since they have come to Him as sinners and trusted His Son as their Savior, they will always be His children. Nothing can ever change that. But God is not always proud of the way they act. Unfortunately, what His people do affects how others feel about Him. Sometimes He has to discipline His children using whatever is necessary to get their attention. Do you remember how you felt when Carol strayed from the closeness of your family? That's how He feels when His children go astray. That's also why in the Bible He compares them to sheep—they sure can be wayward at times.

Diana, you mentioned your attorney friend and the comment he made about working with Christians. I regret his bad experience as well. Apparently, though, he is an attorney you and Brad both respect. I don't need to tell you that many people would call him the exception, not the norm. Attorneys are not always noted for being the most trustworthy segment of the American population. Just as there are good and bad attorneys, there are good and bad Christians. And the fact that there are bad attorneys who nevertheless are attorneys parallels the fact that there are bad Christians who nevertheless are Christians. Please don't let hypocrites and their deplorable lifestyles keep you from believing the greatest message you've ever heard.

But Diana, you are overlooking the most important thing of all. God is not asking you to trust Christians. They cannot take you to heaven. The most perfect Christian cannot forgive your sins and save you. God is asking you to trust Jesus Christ. He was not a hypocrite. After all, hypocrites don't die on a cross for you. Even the soldiers who crucified Him never found one thing wrong with anything He did. Please don't let Christians keep you from doing what you need to do. Even though they may disappoint you, Christ won't.

One more thing. You mentioned the Christian friend who said that if you came to Christ, all your troubles would be behind you. She meant well, but that's not true. Actually, you will have some new problems, particularly when your brother, Ned, finds out. From what you've told me, you'll be in for some real ridicule from him. He probably won't be as close to you as he is now. He will be convinced that his little sister has gone off the deep end. What your friend was really trying to tell you is that you will have Christ, and He's bigger than any problem you could have. If you let Him, He'll show you how to live the most satisfying and fulfilling life you've ever known, the kind that will impress others and make them ask about God. In many ways, I have more problems now than before I came to Christ. But problems don't seem to be as big as they used to be because He's there with me. There is a calmness and peace in my life that is hard to describe. It sure has made a difference for me. That's why I want this so much for you.

Thanks for listening, Diana. Please carefully consider what I've shared, and let's talk again.

Marsha

Ricardo's Struggle

I asked God to prove his existence to me
by helping me with my problems.
I'm still waiting for him to do so.

Who Is Ricardo?

Ricardo is divorced and remarried, and lives in North Carolina. He works for a company that produces industrial supplies. A very pragmatic thinker, he's more emotional than some men. He is also extremely experience-oriented and thinks of life in terms of the "here and now" and not the hereafter. (His thoughts are almost always on today and tomorrow instead of what is going to happen after he dies.) Part of this is because recently life for Ricardo has been a continual struggle to make ends meet and to keep everything right-side-up.

Listening to Ricardo

Dear Steve,

There is a lot I could be criticized for. I'm irritable around my wife, I yell at my kids, and I go halfheartedly about my job. Everything, from my attitude to my actions, leaves a lot to be desired.

But the one thing I will tell you is that I gave God a chance.

Are you aware that about a year ago my whole world began crumbling? First, I got word that my brother had been killed in a car crash in Seattle. He's the only person I've ever been very close to, probably because he's the only one I've ever felt cared about me. I no sooner returned from his funeral than I got word of our company's layoffs, and, a month later, I was out of work. Then, as if that wasn't enough, one morning I woke up with a pain in my chest. Because heart disease is very prevalent on my dad's side of the family, I spent a terrifying week before I had the nerve to go to a doctor. It turned out to be nothing serious, but it sure had me worried. I'd really believed I was on the verge of a heart attack. All this was during a time when my wife and I were having some serious discussions about splitting up. As you're aware, I'd already gone through one divorce. We've decided now to stick it out until the kids are grown, but we both realize we made a big mistake in getting married. As we look back on it, since we both came from broken marriages, we probably came together out of hurt, not love. We're as opposite as opposites can be.

During this time, I got on my knees. My wife still doesn't know it, but I figured she didn't need to. It was probably my ego that kept me from telling her. I asked God if he was for real and, if he was, could he help me with my problems and prove himself to me. I never heard from him. There have been times when I've not always been sincere, but that wasn't one of them. I was as serious as I could be. In fact, there were days I was so low I wished for death. Then there were other days I was scared to death to die.

At work the other day, a fellow in my department and I were dumping our problems on each other. He's going through some serious things right now. He said he tried praying, too, and felt like he was talking to a wall. He says he's an atheist now.

Does God have a list of those he likes and those he doesn't like? If so, am I just not on the "I like you" list? I can't figure it out. I came to him when I was really down and gave him a chance. He had an opportunity to sign me up, but he didn't. Why?

The way I see it, God just seems to be a major disappointment. The more I think about it, the more I realize I'm becoming an atheist, too.

Ricardo

Looking at Ricardo

Ricardo's open expression of disappointment in God is a big advantage. It allows Steve to be just as open with Ricardo. At the same time, Steve has to come across as being on Ricardo's team, not on his back.

Ricardo is so experience-oriented, he measures God on that basis. Because of this he's missed entirely the message of Christ's death and resurrection. In addition, when an experience in which God has been good to him fades into the background, he's dissatisfied without a new one to take its place.

He must be shown what Christ has done for him through His substitutionary death and resurrection. Even if God had come to his rescue during his "down" moments, that would not have changed Ricardo's eternal destiny. To get everything in proper perspective, Ricardo must focus on what Christ has already done for him, not what He might do. Every day Ricardo is paid to labor with his hands. He doesn't need to think deeply about his work. That plays a part in his not thinking more deeply about Jesus Christ. Just because he hasn't needed to apply himself in that way before doesn't mean he cannot be challenged to do so.

Two things could be used by God to penetrate Ricardo's defenses. First, it cannot be emphasized too strongly that he must focus on what Christ did for him on a cross. If he does not come face to face with that, he'll never be able to make a genuine decision for Christ because he'll never see his lost condition. Secondly, Ricardo has to see, on a tangible daily basis, how good God has been to him. That knowledge will help his experience-oriented thinking and could bring him to see a side of God he's completely overlooked.

Responding to Ricardo

Dear Ricardo,

Please don't worry whether or not you're on the list of people God likes. In fact, I'd prefer you use the word love because that expresses His feelings toward you and everyone else. He doesn't just like people, He loves them—including you!

We have a very candid relationship. This is the way it ought to be. You've been open with me, so allow me to be open with you. The truth is, God has proven Himself to you.

Let's start with the greatest proof of all—proof that even your friends who profess to be atheists (and, by the way, God loves them, too) have not been able to deny. For thirty-three years God's Son, Jesus Christ, walked on the earth. Never once was He found guilty of any wrongdoing. The reason was because He never sinned. He was absolutely perfect. But God allowed Him to be punished for all of your sins, all of my sins, and all of everybody else's sins. That way, through punishing Christ for what you and I have done, He could forgive us and give us life eternal.

What happened on the third day after Jesus Christ died? He rose again proving that He had conquered sin and could offer eternal life to all who would trust Him as their personal Savior. Not one person has ever been able to disprove that empty tomb. God's Son is alive and real. The resurrection is all the proof anyone needs. It is one of the most documented facts of history. A supernatural resurrection is the only explanation for the empty tomb. That empty tomb is a fact—one that has brought many people to Christ. There isn't a single person I know who has approached the empty tomb with an open mind without coming to Him. What more proof could you ask for?

I don't think you are as close to becoming an atheist as you may think. You simply haven't experienced God as real in your own life. Wouldn't that be an accurate way to put it? But, Ricardo, even if you were a person who was totally convinced that there is no God, you would owe it to yourself to try to disprove the resurrection.

I know what you're about to say: "But that happened about two thousand years ago." You tend to focus on things in the present, not in the past. Sure, it happened a long time ago. But the resurrection is the basis on which God can ask every person to come as a sinner and trust Christ as his or her personal Savior. God's Son suffered death in your place and arose on the third day. The proof is there. The resurrection is a historical fact, and it proves He's for real. I cannot emphasize that enough. The resurrection is like a billboard that shouts to the world, "Jesus Christ is alive."

Could I caution you on something? I don't mean to offend you. You have a weakness most of us have, myself included. We see only the side we're looking for in people. For example, my father-in-law has a lot of fine qualities, but I often overlook them. If I'm not careful, I see only the bad side of him. Sometimes, all I notice is his short fuse, and it bothers me. Similarly, if you try to find a negative side of God, although there is none, you'll probably think you've found something. In doing so, you overlook everything He's done for you.

You have two handsome sons. You care for them so much that you and your wife are "sticking it out for them." Have you ever asked yourself, "Why should God bless me with these two boys?" You've told me you feel as if you don't deserve them. Go back to that period when you were out of work. It was a hard time, but your family didn't miss a single meal. You even remarked to Cassandra, "I don't know how we made it, but we did." Within six months, you had another job—one that came to you "out of the blue." Can't you see God's goodness in that? One thing after another adds up to the fact that He loves you.

God cannot be manipulated or used. When you got down on your knees and asked Him to prove Himself to you, you wanted temporary assistance. You were going through a lot of struggles and really felt the weight of them. But God's not interested in giving temporary assistance. He loves you so much He wants to save you from eternal punishment and give you eternal life. He will do that for you today if you acknowledge your need, recognize what His Son did for you, and trust in

Him to save you. Think about it. You have never had a problem like the one you're facing right now—the same one everybody faces: eternal separation from Him because of your sins. That is the problem that must be addressed. Jesus Christ addressed it by dying in your place as your substitute. All He's asking is for you to accept what He has done for you.

Once you come to Christ and start growing as a Christian, you will discover the same thing millions of others have. When you have Him in your life, your problems don't seem as bad. The reason is that He's become a part of your life, and He's bigger than any troubles you have. I know that at times you're frustrated with just about everything. But if you come to Christ, I promise on the basis of both the Bible and personal experience, not only will you be certain of life in the hereafter but also you'll have happiness and contentment in the here and now unlike anything you've ever known. That is why Christians often say about Christ, "He adds years to your life and life to your years."

Look at your uncle. You know that his life has been nothing but hardships. He's suffered the deaths of two wives, he's had difficulties raising a son with muscular dystrophy, and he's had more than one financial setback due to circumstances beyond his control. Then last year his house was burglarized. Despite all this, he never changes—you've seen that. He focuses on how he can lift others up, not on how they can lift him up. It's because he knows Christ and lives very closely to Him. There is no hardship he has gone through which he hasn't had God's strength to help him handle. When I first started talking to you about the Lord, you said it bothered you because you've heard it all before from your uncle. I'm glad we know each other better now, and we can talk more. But the only reason either of us "pesters" you is because we're concerned about you.

If you come to Christ, it has to be on His terms—recognizing your eternally lost condition and your need of a Savior. He's not just a button you push when there's an emergency.

I feel I've gone right to the point about things. Please don't be offended. I value our friendship. I want you to see how God has already proven Himself to you, though perhaps not in the way you'd like Him to. Let's talk some more.

Steve

Ann's Struggle

My husband, Brent, died last year.
If I come to Christ, I will have to accept
the fact that Brent is in hell.
Admitting that is extremely difficult.

Who Is Ann?

Ann was the wife of a retired dairy farmer in Wisconsin. Her husband died of leukemia a year ago. Only now, through the witness of two people God has brought across her path, has she begun to think about spiritual things. Although she understands the gospel, coming to Christ has some serious consequences in her mind.

Listening to Ann

Dear Adria,

My emotions are so mixed up that I don't know how to sort them all out. I am angry, bitter, remorseful, distressed, and overwhelmed. And each day is getting harder, not easier.

At least you will talk to me. My friend Denise, who is so put out with me that she probably won't ever talk to me again, said, "Religious people are the hardest to reach." I don't doubt that she's right. I have gone to church all my life, taught Sunday school, and sung in the choir. All the time, I thought I was stacking up brownie points that would give me a better chance at heaven than most people. The church I belong to doesn't study the Bible, so I had never seen what I recently learned—that God cannot let me into heaven based on church attendance. The paragraph that she showed me in the eighteenth chapter of Luke about the Pharisee and the tax collector really startled me. But even if I had seen it earlier, I probably would have been too stubborn to listen. I think Brent's passing was a wake-up call.

That's a good way to put it: a wake-up call. I see it now like never before. No amount of religion will get me into heaven, but because God's perfect Son, Jesus, died for me on a cross, taking all the punishment I deserved, God can accept me based on Christ's payment for my sins. If I trust Christ as my Savior, because of his death and resurrection I can receive eternal life free. There are still times that it sounds too good to be true. I have been so lonely and miserable since Brent died, I'm sure that's what has made me more open. I have needed someone to talk to, and just before I met you, Denise was that friend. I think if Brent hadn't been taken so tragically it would have been easier for me. I didn't have any time to prepare myself. It seems as though we found out about the leukemia one day, and he was gone the next.

I'm sure that's why Denise tried to get through my "religiosity" and showed me the first verse I ever learned in Sunday school—John 3:16. It seems so simple: "For God so loved the world that He gave His only begotten Son, that whoever believes in Him should not perish but have everlasting life." You can probably tell that I understand it so well now I could explain it to somebody else. In fact—and this is crazy—the other day I got into an argument with a friend at church over the whole thing. She is convinced that her baptism will save her. But she hasn't read the Bible either.

I know this sounds terrible, but sometimes I wish I had never understood that verse, and that Denise and then you had never shown it to me. I'm not mad at her, and I'm not mad at you either—at least not all the time! I know Brent didn't understand. If I accept what God says in the Bible as truth, I have to face the fact that Brent is probably in hell. I feel sure nobody ever explained to him what Denise explained to me. Sometimes I think I would rather just be in hell with Brent. I know that is probably a terrible thing to say. You don't know what a big problem this is to me. I'm so torn that sometimes I feel if I don't get help, I'll lose my mind.

Ann

Looking at Ann

It is both unbiblical and unethical to give Ann false hope. If her husband trusted Christ, he is in heaven. If he didn't, he isn't. One need not describe the horribleness of hell. That would be the epitome of insensitivity. At the same time, one cannot talk as though hell does not exist or that God might make an exception.

However, there are two things that people in this situation entirely overlook. The first is that if a loved one is in hell, he is hoping the ones he loved will not join him. Nobody in hell would wish hell on anyone else. The story in Luke 16 proves that. The rich man begs Abraham to let Lazarus, who is in such comfort, return to earth and warn his brothers about the place of torment. The non-Christian often grasps this truth when the situation is turned around and the non-Christian is asked, "What if you died first without Christ? Wouldn't you, too, be longing for the people you care about to come to Christ?"

Equally important is the second thing. Non-Christians who have lost a non-Christian loved one normally focus on the past. Rarely do they think of the impact they could have on present or future family members. It is better for them to accept the loss of one person than risk being separated from all their loved ones. This thought can help them see not only their own need of Christ but also the need to be a bearer of good news to the rest of their family. The future, therefore, gives us an opportunity to talk to them about accepting the message of Christ's death and resurrection and communicating that message to others.

Here is an opportunity for warmth, understanding, and truth to come together and result in the spiritual rebirth of the lost.

The person will have the excitement and certainty of knowing that when she dies she'll be with Christ. She'll have the certainty that while on earth Christ will be with her. The non-Christian who is struggling with burdens that seem overwhelming needs to understand that one evidence of Christ's love for us is His desire to help us with those burdens. She needs to know that the last day before she comes to Christ is the last day she ever faces life alone!

Most people come to Christ in the midst of a change—the loss of a job, a geographical move that separates them from family and friends, a health problem, a divorce, or something as difficult as the loss of a close family member through death. We have to be careful in dealing with such people and assist them in making an intelligent decision, not simply an emotional choice. If these lost people are properly and patiently dealt with, God could use the unsettling changes to bring them to Christ.

Responding to Ann

Dear Ann,

I am glad you wrote. I've known you a only short time, but you're such an easy person to get close to. Please talk to me about anything you need to—even the things you find hard to discuss.

There is something that I hadn't understood until I was a Christian for about five years. Denise did not come across your path by accident, and I didn't either. God wants everybody to come to Him, so He brings people and situations into our lives to get us thinking.

As Denise told you, religious people are often the hardest to reach. Even Jesus Christ had more difficulty reaching the religious people of His time than anyone else. If anyone ever spoke to Brent about Christ, that may have been what kept him from listening. To religious people, Christians often seem like religious fanatics. Brent prided himself on all he did for the church you both attended. There is no question about it, he did a lot. He was one of the most kindhearted people I've ever met. But as you have discovered, good deeds do not merit us acceptance with God. I'm glad you now understand that.

I wish so much that somehow I could tell you Brent is in heaven, but I can't. It may be that someone who visited him just before he died shared the gospel with him and he came to Christ. Even if He embraced the Savior thirty seconds before he died, he's in the presence of Jesus Christ right now. But I don't know if that happened, and I couldn't live with my own conscience if I gave you false hope. However, there are some things you're overlooking that will be helpful to think about.

Brent loved you. In the little time I knew him before he died, I could tell you were everything to him. Suppose he is not in heaven. Think about it, Ann. The one thing he would beg you to do now is to accept God's Son's punishment for your sins instead of suffering your own punishment. There's not a day that goes by that he isn't pleading for you to come to Christ and enjoy His free gift of eternal life. I know you haven't thought about that, but you need to. Suppose you had died first without Christ. Would you not be pleading for Brent to come to Him? So if you want what God, Brent, Denise, and I want, you ought to trust Christ as your Savior.

There is another thing you don't realize, and it could comfort you. When you come to Christ, any problem of yours is a problem of His. That means you won't carry your burdens alone. He is there with you, and all of a sudden you have the strength to go on from day to day, strength that you never had before. It's one thing for me to explain it to you, but it's another thing when you experience it for yourself.

When my daughter, Caroline, was only eight years old, I saw her lifting her heavy toy box. I couldn't believe she was trying to do that, and I was afraid she'd hurt herself. I immediately took one end of the box, and in no time the two of us had it in the other room. It was such a little thing, but the two of us still laugh about it. At the time, she said, "Wow, Mom. You made it a lot easier." That's how it is when Christ is in your life. Each burden is a bit easier to bear when He is there with you to help you carry it.

How does this relate to Brent's death? His separation from God is a burden you would no longer carry by yourself. The Lord would be there with you every moment of every day. That is a promise, and He doesn't break promises. One of the first verses I learned after I became a Christian was 1 Peter 5:7, which says, "Casting all your care upon Him, for He cares for you." I needed that verse at the time because of the cancer scare we were going through with my mother. With God's help, you would be able to face every day, go on with your life, and not be overwhelmed by your grief. Before I came to Christ, I never knew how personally concerned He is about everything in my life. That verse has meant everything to me.

Speaking of my daughter, Caroline, let's talk about your children. Because of your grief for Brent, you are dwelling in the past. You can't keep looking back, Ann. You have to look ahead. You have three children and two grandchildren, all of whom don't understand what I've explained to you. They love and respect you, and rightly so—you have been very loving to them. There is nothing you wouldn't do for them. You're the "supermom and super grandmother." I know you hate the thought that Brent may not be in heaven, and so do I. But you don't want your children and grandchildren to be separated from God, too. If you come to Christ, He could use you to lead each one of them to Him. They would probably listen to you because of the love and respect they have for you. He has brought entire families to Himself, and, using your voice, He could help your family understand as well. Again, you have to look ahead and not just behind.

I love you, Ann. Think about all of this. I'll be out your way this weekend; let's talk some more. I really think you are very close to getting it all settled. I want that more than you will ever know.

Adria

Claire's Struggle

Okay, you're getting through to me.
But I'm scared to death that if I trust
Christ, he'll want me to be a missionary
in Africa. I'm just not cut out for that.

Who Is Claire?

Claire lives in a suburb of Washington, D.C., and serves as an accountant in a rapidly growing engineering firm. Single and secure, she enjoys her freedom as well as her luxuries. Her biggest struggle, as she contemplates a relationship with God, is fear of what He might require her to do. But not coming to Christ scares her as much as what coming to Him might mean.

Listening to Claire

Dear Susan,

I'm enjoying that women's Bible study you invited me to, and for the first time I think I understand what God is about. I had the same problem a lot of people do. I always figured that the harder you worked the better your chances were of getting into heaven. When our friend Natalie told me that eternal life was a free gift, I told her, "Nothing is free!" After discussing it with her for an hour, I started to understand. I'll never forget when she showed me a verse in Ephesians. I read it so many times that I have it embedded in my memory: "For by grace you have been saved through faith, and that not of yourselves; it is the gift of God." Suddenly, it seemed as if a light had come on. God is offering eternal life as a free gift because his Son died in my place. Since Jesus Christ took the punishment that I should have had and rose on the third day, God can forgive me all my wrongs and give me heaven free. That has to be the neatest thing I have ever heard! If anything is an expression of love, that's it. Natalie could tell that I understood. She invited me to place my trust in Christ to save me, but I told her I wasn't ready, and I'm not. I feel that God is trying to tell me I need to come to him by the people and circumstances he is bringing into my life, but I'm even less ready now than I was before.

Here is my problem, and I still can't tell Natalie. She is such a good persuader, I'm afraid she will ask me to face my fears, and I'm not ready to do that. You don't come on quite as strong, and I feel a little more comfortable talking to you. I might eventually come to God but not right now. Back in high school, my best friend, Tracy, became a Christian. I didn't understand what had happened. I'm still not sure I do. Immediately, all of her plans changed. She was headed into modeling because she had the face and the figure for it. Before I knew it, however, she was talking about Africa. She said she wanted to be a missionary, and even her boyfriend, who was about to become her fiancé, dropped her. When I tried to talk her out of it, she said she had heard a missionary at her church. What he said to her made sense, so she felt moved to sign up. I didn't see her for five years, and then she called me out of the blue. She was back home visiting her family and wanted me to meet her husband. I'll admit they both seemed happy, even though he was no Prince Charming.

I'm scared that is what God will want me to do. Under no circumstances am I interested. I'm just not cut out for that. So I have to say thanks, but no thanks. I'm sticking to my job as an accountant here in Washington, D.C. I've decided to stop searching. I hope you understand. It's just not for me.

Claire

Looking at Claire

Claire has made the mistake many other people make. She's confusing two things: entering the Christian life and living the Christian life. To put it another way, she has confused salvation and discipleship. If we can help her think clearly in both areas, as the Holy Spirit works in her, Claire might see her need of Christ.

If Claire doesn't see that the love of God has no strings attached, she still hasn't comprehended the grace of God. The grace of God is such that He says, "I love you, period" not "I love you if." Claire has to understand this; otherwise, salvation and service lose the distinctiveness they are given in Scripture. Both are important, but if they are confused or mingled, salvation is thought to be on the basis of Christ plus works, not on Christ alone.

At the same time, we don't want to give Claire the idea that if she comes to Christ she doesn't need to care what God thinks about her life. That idea is unbiblical, and it could cause Claire to miss out on something fantastic: the joy of a life completely surrendered to Christ.

That's why Claire has to see discipleship the way Scripture presents it—as a powerful yes. It's a life in which we realize our full potential. Since Claire is a "go-getter" and wants her life to count, she could be helped to see that only God knows how her life could count the most. If Christ's saving grace is properly presented to her, Claire could come to see that Tracy was a very smart person who made a very smart decision.

Notice, Claire hasn't realized that Susan is equally dedicated to Christ. The "He'll want me to be a missionary" thing is so troubling to her that she doesn't see what Susan is doing. Susan could easily feel that Claire thinks of Tracy as being a better Christian than she is herself. This would be foolish since Claire is a non-Christian who, unless God dispels her blindness, will see only what Satan allows her to see. But what an opportunity for Susan to explain why she enjoys serving God where she is and how she feels confident that she is right in the middle of God's will for her life.

Claire's words belie what she says about deciding to stop her search. She knows enough about the love of God that backing off wouldn't be easy. She concedes that what she has come to understand about Christ is very appealing to her. Patience and honesty could make the difference with Claire.

Responding to Claire

Dear Claire,

One of the things I like about you is that you say what you're thinking. With you "what you see is what you get." But, Claire, you are confusing a whole bunch of things. Since I've taken the time to listen to you, it's your turn to listen to me. Fair enough?

I'm glad Natalie helped you understand the major message of the Bible. That is where people have to start. Until they see that God is offering a free gift because of what His Son, Jesus Christ, did for them through His death and resurrection, they will not understand. It is so simple. That is why many miss the message. Most people say exactly what you said to Natalie: "Nothing is free."

But you're also saying something that God is not saying. His message is "I love you—period!" It is not "I love you—if." Talk to Tracy. God never told her He would accept her only if she would be a missionary in Africa. Tracy chose to be a missionary. He never told her that He wouldn't save her unless she made Him a promise first.

I can tell from what you have told me about Tracy that everything changed when she came to Christ. She knew beyond any doubt that she was going to spend eternity with God. But why did Tracy become a missionary? When you understand why, it will remove your confusion. If you remember, you introduced her to me that time she was home visiting her family. We had about half an hour to talk while you were on the phone. She explained just about everything. As you know, she's so excited about her life that she opens up easily.

As soon as Tracy came to Christ, she started to grow as a Christian. You know how enthusiastic she is when she discovers something she knows is right. And as she grew, she decided she wanted to be what the Bible calls a disciple, someone who says to God, "Here's my life. Do with it as you please." Tracy told me she felt God could do more with her life than she could. You were right about the missionary who spoke in her church and how his message affected her whole future. That's one of the first things she told me. But did she ever tell you what it was he said that affected her so strongly?

He made one comment that she couldn't get out of her mind: "Everybody you meet is facing eternity. The only question is where they will spend it. What are you doing to make a difference?" Suddenly, money, things, popularity, and fame didn't matter to her anymore. She wanted to live for other people and not for herself. She told me that she kept saying to herself, "If I could lead someone else to Christ, the way my friend led me to Him, that would be worth living for." That was when her dream of modeling ended. And you're right. She is gorgeous. It's not hard to envy her. But Tracy didn't want to come to the end of her life and say, "I was a model." That seemed so empty. To come to the end of her life and say, "I introduced people to Christ" meant everything. Since this missionary talked about needing more people to spread the gospel, Tracy signed up voluntarily. God never told her that He wouldn't accept her if she didn't become a missionary. He's certainly not telling you that. It was her decision. Could she have served God in the right circumstances as a model? Of course she could have. There is no doubt about it. But that just wasn't for her.

Claire, do me a favor. Jump ahead a hundred years. When

Tracy is with Christ, a lot of other people whom she led to Christ will be there in heaven with her. Can you imagine how satisfying and fulfilling that will be? That is what will make the impact of her life lasting and not temporary.

When someone comes to Christ and then says, "Show me how my life can count," He does that. Think of Todd, the guy you so admired when your family was in North Carolina. His construction company is one of the most respected in the state. Todd puts Christ in the very center of his business. He makes less money than many contractors because he uses a lot of his time helping churches in his community. Your dad even mentioned to me the other day how impressed he is by Todd's generosity. Now there is a Christian who is having an impact on eternity. Just like Tracy, he is living for what counts, not for what doesn't count. Do you understand?

God refuses to offer you eternal life with strings attached. He loves you—period. If you trust Christ today to save you, He will freely give you eternal life. Why don't you do that? You don't have to promise to be a missionary in Africa before you come to Him. Once you have come to Him and learn more about Him, He will help you decide how your life can count so you can invest your years on earth and not just spend them as most people do. You will learn the same thing Tracy has. God knows where you fit in life better than you do. With the abilities He has given you, there are some exciting ways He can use you, and I'm convinced you will have no regrets. Don't you realize that Tracy could come home today if she wanted to? Nobody, including God Himself, is keeping her from coming home. But Africa is where she wants to be. It can be explained in one sentence: With Christ she has found out what is important and what is not. He would like to help you see the same thing.

Speaking of direction for your life, Christ could even help you think through what you need to look for in a husband—something I gather you are very confused about. Knowing Christ not only settles your eternal destiny but also gives you direction here and now.

Claire, God must have known I wasn't cut out to do what Tracy does. I have given my life to Christ, and I don't feel called to be a missionary in Africa. I've simply never felt that is where He wants me. But I love my position at the computer firm. God gives me a chance to smile at everybody I meet—something that seems to astound people. In fact, the other day a coworker invited me to lunch. She is going through a pretty traumatic divorce, and I think she wants to do some serious talking. I sure hope so because I want to help. That's why I feel God has me here. I feel I'm as surrendered to Him as Tracy is. He uses all of us where He knows we fit the best. For right now, there is no question in my mind that He wants me here.

You said you're going to stop searching. Claire, if you do, that will be without question the biggest mistake you'll ever make. Please don't tune God out.

Instead, let's keep talking. We need to—not just for your sake but for mine. You mean so much to me. You know I'm not going to pressure you. I'll just help you keep thinking. After all, Claire, some people think you're the best, and I'm one of them!

Susan

Part 3

Three Final Observations

Three Final Observations

Evangelism isn't easy. If you ever meet someone who says it is, his feet have never touched earth! At the same time, it's not nearly as difficult as we often make it.

If I could offer three final observations on our witness to the lost, it would be the following.

Concentrate on listening and thinking before responding. Non-Christians don't always express what they're feeling. Sometimes their words only hint at what they are really trying to say. At other times, they are expressing their feelings. Regardless, they need someone who will listen with an open ear and a caring heart. It's your listening even more than your talking that tells them, "Here is somebody who wants to know what's going on in my life and what's on my mind." That listening spirit often gives you the opportunity and the credibility to respond lovingly, directly, and with "grace and truth." Not only that, but listening also provides the assurance that you are responding to the needs of non-Christians, not simply to their words.

Keep the message of the gospel in the foreground, not in the background. The message the non-Christian needs most should not be the message they hear last. That message, as God defined it and Paul the apostle declared it, is simply, "Christ died for our sins and rose again." That is why someone who is one day old in Christ can speak to anyone else about the Lord. God never asks, "Do you know the Bible?" He simply asks, "Do you know the gospel?" If someone understands the simple message of Christ's death and resurrection, that person is able to talk to anybody anywhere about the Savior. Those who have been Christians for a long time are often the ones who so quickly get away from the simple message. The facts of His death and resurrection are the issues a lost person must confront. Because He died for us and rose again, we may, through simple trust in Christ, receive His free gift of life eternal.

Don't forget the value of a compliment. Mark Twain reportedly said, "I have never met a person who cannot handle a compliment." I haven't, either. I've noticed that compliments seem to do two things. They put the focus on the non-believer, not on you. That's where the focus needs to be. Second, compliments have a way of saying, "There are some things right about you." That is extremely accurate. There may be plenty of things that are wrong in the lives of non-Christians, but that never means that they aren't doing some things right. Even their willingness to ask and answer questions is something that can be commended—a commendation that could open a door for the gospel.

Unless the Holy Spirit brings non-Christians to Christ, they will never come. We are only instruments, not the power. That is why our prayers on behalf of those who are lost are so important. But if we bear these three things in mind, we can be more effective instruments for the Savior. We can be used by Him to populate heaven. And I repeat, "If that is not exciting, please tell me what is!"

Part 4

Are You Uncertain of Your Eternal Destiny?

Are You Uncertain of Your Eternal Destiny?

If on reading this book you are uncertain of your eternal destiny, now is the time to receive God's free gift. Admit to Him that you are a sinner and place your trust in Christ alone. Christ died for you and rose on the third day. Trusting in Him guarantees you eternal life. Here is how to tell God in a simple prayer what you are doing.

> Dear God,
>   I come to you now. I admit I'm a sinner. There's nothing I can do to be worthy of heaven. I understand that Jesus Christ died on the cross for me and then rose on the third day. I place my trust in Christ alone as my personal Savior. Thank you for the free gift of eternal life. In Jesus' name,
>   Amen

Once you have come to trust Christ, read and memorize John 5:24 which says, "Most assuredly, I say to you, he who hears My word and believes in Him who sent Me has everlasting life, and shall not come into judgment, but has passed from death into life."

Begin growing as a Christian by spending time with Him each day in prayer. Read the Bible. A good place for you to start is the book of Philippians in the New Testament. Begin attending a Bible-believing church. Once you have trusted Christ, you are His forever.

About EvanTell

Declaring the Gospel, clearly and simply
Activating believers around the world
Preparing the next generation to reach the lost

We're passionate about the lost—and reaching them with the gospel. Our programs help believers confidently communicate the gospel—Jesus Christ died for your sins and rose from the dead. EvanTell's ministry outreaches, evangelistic resources, live training workshops, video training curriculum and follow-up materials are built on years of evangelistic experience. Founded in 1973, the ministry was started by Dr. R. Larry Moyer out of a commitment and desire to see the gospel clearly presented with a careful handling of Scripture and a core doctrine of grace.

The Gospel. Clear and Simple.*

EvanTell, Inc.
P.O. Box 741417
Dallas, TX 75374
800.947.7359
www.evantell.org